Seaside's Rock 'n' Roll Riots 1962-1964

How a Coastal City's Labor Day Riots Heralded

a Decade Of Unrest

R. J. MARX

Seaside's Rock 'n' Roll Riots 1962-1964
How A Coastal City's Labor Day Riots Heralded a Decade of Unrest

Copyright © 2024
R.J. Marx
Cover to Cover Publishing
All rights reserved
ISBN 978-09711626-4-8

Table of Contents

Preface	1
End of the Trail	3
A change at the top	8
Chief's firing leads to brouhaha	13
Youth Crackdown	19
Dragging the Gut	24
Riot Day One	31
How rock 'n' roll quelled a riot	41
'The Day After' in Seaside	48
Inquiry into a riot	52
'The Big Blow'	57
How to avoid a riot	62
Fort Seaside	67
Showdown in Seaside	75
Tower down – Again	77
'Wolf Packs' on Broadway	80
Monday, Sept. 2, 1963	86
Blame Game	89
Kids in shiny Caddies	94
'Line in the Sand'	99
A Bid for Harmony	105
Of National Concern	112
The Good Friday Quake	116
'Police power'	121

MOTLEY CREW	125
WHO THREW THE TEAR GAS INTO THE PYPO CLUB?	135
'REMEDIES' FOR A RIOT	138
BLACK RIOTS, WHITE RIOTS	143
THE PEOPLE HAVE SPOKEN	150
EPILOGUE	154
SELECTED BIBLIOGRAPHY	159
ACKNOWLEDGMENTS	161
ABOUT THE AUTHOR	162

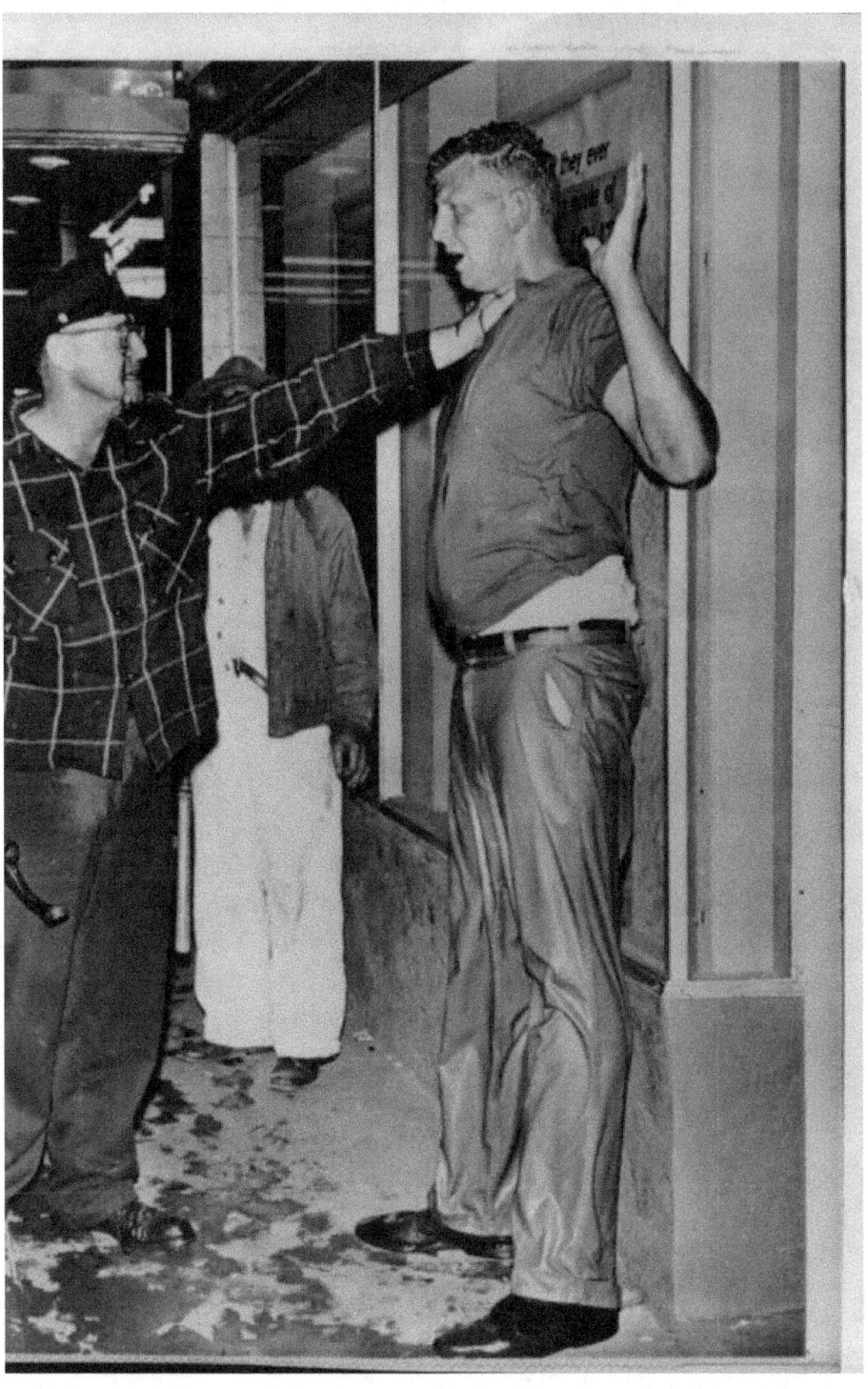

Award-winning photo by the *Oregonian's* Chuck Von Wald shows Seaside volunteer firefighter Hugh McKenna with a grip on a young man on Sept. 1, 1962.

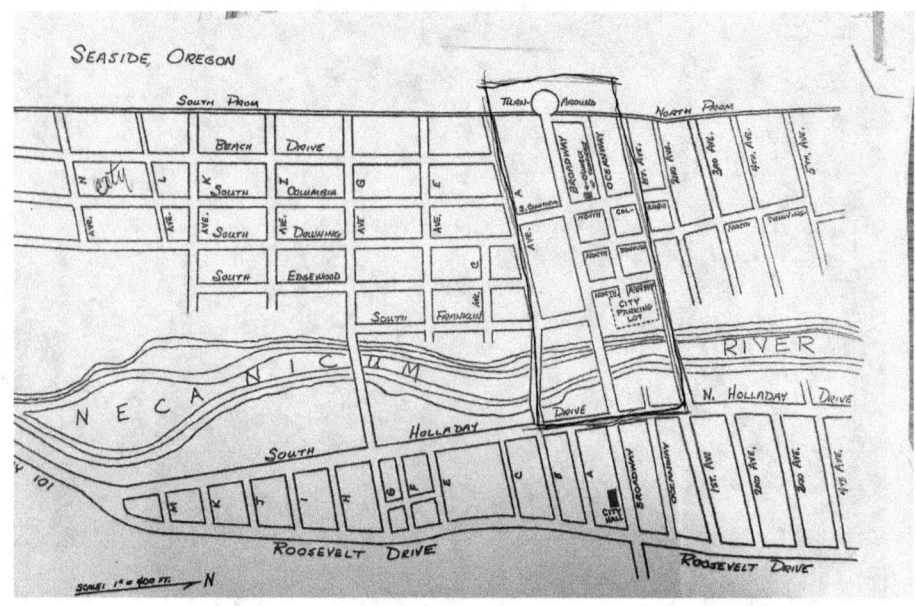

Street map of downtown Seaside, 1960s.

PREFACE

Seaside, Oregon mirrored every American small-town in the 1950s and 1960s: fiercely patriotic, independent yet community minded. Its uniqueness came with its location, far from the city but near, perched at the edge of the continental United States, only 90 minutes by car from the Willamette Valley and three hours from Seattle.

As its Native American population dwindled, Seaside's 19th century settlers were explorers, farmers, visionaries and dreamers, from the locomotive king Ben Holladay Seaside downtown developer Alexandre Gilbert. Oregon's public beaches, guaranteed by Governor Oswald West in 1912, assured that the four miles of waterfront would accessible to everyone.

Along with the visitors came the entrepreneurs, shop owners and professionals needed to make the city thrive. Loggers made a good wage harvesting the abundant timber that covered the nearby hills. Cranberry farmers, orchards, dairies, horse ranches and even mink farms brought many more.

In the late '50s, the term generation gap was just around the corner. American youth, provided what appeared to be unlimited opportunity and wealth, defying their parents, rebels without a cause, wild ones. Hollywood filmmakers inspired fear, featuring biker gangs invading small towns. Rock 'n' roll was their anthem, music that no one over 30 could understand. The kids loved their music loud and they loved that their parents hated it.

"What's the matter with kids today?" the fictional character famously sang in 1958's Broadway hit "Bye Bye Birdie."

Seaside parents wondered that themselves as they watched their resort community transformed in those years by a steady stream of young people packing into hotel rooms, pitching tents on the beach, or hitching rides back to wherever.

Over Labor Day weekends in 1962, 1963, and 1964, those kids asserted themselves in a way they hadn't before. They gathered en masse on downtown Seaside's main street of Broadway, partying, fighting, drinking and dancing. Their presence drew law enforcement, arrests, injuries and international headlines. A worried nation asked, "Where are we headed?"

Seaside found itself on the map in a way it never intended.

I moved to Seaside in 2015 and even now, in 2024, have found that people are still assessing the effects of those three tumultuous years.

Seaside's Rock 'n' Roll Riots 1962-1964 examines the events leading up to the riots and how the city responded to three years of violent clashes that changed the course of the city forever.

Seaside's Turnaround, an ever-popular tourist attraction, as seen in the 1960s.

END OF THE TRAIL

The years of Seaside's Labor Day riots – 1962, 1963 and 1964 – could be characterized as a mash-up of beach movie, national youth unrest, with a hefty dose of small-town City Hall drama.

Seaside was the final stop of the Lewis and Clark Expedition westward – the Corps of Discovery. In the winter of 1805-1806, Captain Meriwether Lewis and Second Lieutenant William Clark sent a detachment to the sand beach 20 miles south of their Astoria encampment, the so-called "end of the trail." Their job was to boil down enough ocean salt to supply the corps for the return trip east.

A century later, the visitors from the burgeoning Portland metropolitan area began to arrive in Seaside. With rail service connecting the Willamette Valley to the Coast, families made the journey and spent their summers in the oceanside community. They rented cabins and bungalows; families enjoyed the beach, camped, rode horses and swam at the natatorium. They enjoyed the options downtown, miniature golf, bumper cars or amusement rides. Fathers came on weekends on what was to be called "The Daddy Train," dropped off in a herd of summer finery at the locomotive's final stop in Seaside. In early years they could see horse racing on the south end of town; hunters could find unlimited bounty on nearby Saddle Mountain.

Later they could golf or hobnob with friends at one of the city's many fraternal organizations — among them, the Elks, the Moose and the Legion.

After the repeal of alcohol prohibition in 1933, the town soon had "more saloons than churches," one observed recalled. "And there were a lot of churches!"

Later they would put on the ritz with dinner at the Crab Broiler or the Par-Tee Club, white napkin establishments that drew visitors from all over. Complemented by the social swirl of neighboring Gearhart to the north and the laid-back Bohemianism of Gearhart to the south, the coast offered something for everyone.

Despite a climate that often brought 10 months of rain, Seaside's local year-round population swelled with farmers, fishermen and loggers. Hawkers, hoteliers salesmen, entertainers and impresarios arrived to take advantage of the bustling community.

Abundant natural resources — timber, stone quarries, farmland — brought laborers to the coast for seasonal or year-round jobs. Professionals followed to provide legal, accounting and medical services. Retirees found vacation bargains and a comfortable respite by the sea without the rush and clamor of the big cities they had toiled in for decades of their working lives.

Seaside is perched perilously in the tsunami inundation zone; geologists reckon the city could be destroyed even after a medium-size earthquake and subsequent tidal wave. The threat had yet to be recognized; most people didn't even hear the word until the Alaska quake and tsunami of 1964.

Fabulous '50s

At a reunion in 2018, 1957 and 1958 Seaside High School grads remembered growing up in Seaside as "idyllic."

Sue Ward Lee described the freedom to ride a horse in the hills "all day as long as I got back for dinner."

"My dad and mother just said, 'Be independent.' That was their goal."

Marlene Ordway Laws remembered the same type of upbringing in Cannon Beach.

"It was the same with the Gearhart kids," Judy Wrenn Carder added.

Downtown was much busier then, said Carol deLange Brenneman. "It astounds me when I go downtown in Seaside at this point during the summer at night. It's really quite quiet. You can look down the street and hardly see any cars."

In the 1950s, teens would cruise "around, car to car and car, in order to meet and greet," Brenneman said.

It was so safe in Seaside, "we never did lock a door."

Teens rode their bikes to softball in Gearhart; older high schoolers drove to Gearhart's Sunset Drive-In, located on a 12-acre property north of Gearhart junction, now largely residential. You could play miniature golf at Tiny Tee's, grab a corn dog next door, or play games of chance in Vern's Arcade.

At the same time, Seaside was losing population, with a large number of vacant buildings. When train service stopped coming to Seaside in the early 1950s, fewer families came to Seaside, staying for shorter periods of time. The summer migration became more sporadic; few families in the competitive economy had the resources to spend three months in the country.

Construction during the 1950s was only about half the state average.

By 1955, Seaside's population disproportionately skewed older, with the number of residents over age 65 doubling in population since 1940. Only 28% of the population was 18 or under, compared with the state average of 36%.

High school and college-age visitors to Seaside made up for it. Young people piled into their muscle cars – the Bel Air, Skylarks and Thunderbirds – speeding down the Sunset Highway to make pilgrimages to Seaside over spring break, summer and Labor Day weekends. Others sputtered in retooled jeeps, jalopies and beaters to drive on the beach or into the woods.

They camped on the beach or piled into local motels and cabins, enjoying a relaxed atmosphere and willing to pay the $29.50 fine for public drunkenness. They could listen to rock bands at local clubs, get cheap beer with no questions asked from vendors on the Prom, and head down to the Cove for some of the best surfing anywhere.

Surfin' USA

Jim and Chuck Reed introduced the exotic sport of surfing to Seaside in the 1930s, The Reeds "staked out" Seaside and its big waves at the south end of town by the

Tillamook Head promontory long before it became a national surf destination, family members said.

"Jim supervised the construction of the first real Hawaiian surfboard ever used in Oregon," Melinda Masters, his niece, recalled. "He introduced surfing to Seaside and explained to the public how the surfboard is of considerable value to lifesaving work."

"These were the original 'beach boys,'" Masters' brother, also named Jim Reed, said. "People here did not know what a surfboard was."

But it took Hollywood's myth-makers to make it a fad in the 1950s, to be joyfully portrayed in a string of low-budget beach movies, with daring surfer boys, muscle men, and blonde, bikini-ed Barbie dolls at their side.

'The devil's music'

Seaside wore its dancing shoes as early as the 1920s, when dancers had flocked to the Bungalow one block west of the Promenade at Columbia Street and Broadway. Through the 1930s and 1940s, world-class bandleaders like Duke Ellington, Glenn Miller and Jimmie Lunceford (who died in Seaside before a band date in July 1947) performed and drew fans from Portland, Seattle and beyond.

The Miss Oregon contest established itself in Seaside in 1947 with the crowning of the first state queen, JoAnn Amorde Berg, further establishing itself as the Atlantic City of the West Coast.

Professional wrestling could be seen at the Broadway School, featuring such all-stars as "Wild Bill" Savage, Luther Lindsay and "Tough Tony" Borne.

The main street, Broadway, was crammed with honky-tonks, bars and clubs.

Music could be heard at the Seasider Hotel lounge, the China Doll Lounge in the Cathay Broiler restaurant; live music swung weekends at the Moose Lodge until 1:30 a.m. and at the Elks' Club from 8 p.m. to 2 a.m. Vern Raw Enterprises even piped "mood music" from a studio into "your store, shop or business."

The Pypo Club – pronounced "pie-po," named for a type of small surfboard or "skim board" – was an under-21 music club located in the old American Legion club which was above the Natatorium at the Turnaround.

"It was the place to go in the mid '60s during high school," Seaside's Karen Emmerling told *The Daily Astorian* in 2008. "You had to come to Seaside to go to the Pypo Club.'

A local college student, Gil Tolan, and Seaside High School graduate Joe Camberg hatched the idea for the teens-only nightclub, Seaside's Leah Griffith said.
Steve Johnson, the high school football coach, served as the adult of the trio with the assistance of Oney Camberg, Joe's mother and owners of restaurants in Seaside and along the Sunset Highway near Elsie.
They opened their club at the former American Legion – located at the south end of the Turnaround on Broadway – in the summer of 1961, charging 25 cents admission. They served concoctions like "Seafoam Sluppers" and "Pypo Punches" for a quarter, and soft drinks for 15 cents. Each attendee was breath-tested for signs of alcohol.
The Pypo Club became a hotbed for upcoming bands, including Pacific Northwest standouts like The Fabulous Wailers, the Kingsmen and Paul Revere and the Raiders. The club was a talent incubator, one of a string of venues in the Pacific Northwest to support a new generation of rock 'n' rollers and their fans.
Author Dave Marsh, in his book *Louie Louie: The History and Mythology of the World's Most Famous Rock 'n' Roll Song,* described kids "pumping their quarters" into the club's jukebox to hear the Fabulous Wailers and their version of the hit rock song, "Louie Louie" during the summer of 1961.
"They punched the same button over and over – the one that spat out the Wailers' 'Louie Louie.' As 'duh-duh-duh, duh-duh, filled the room, the crowd danced avidly, shingalinging themselves into a frenzied sweat."
The Wailers' Buck Ormsby told Marsh "young kids turned up regularly, and not all of them on the fringes of teenage society by any means, though the music was still just outlaw enough."
"There were carloads of kids coming," Ormsby said. "It was OK then to go to a dance if you were 15 or 16."
In the pre-Beatles era, parents saw rock 'n' roll as the "devil's music."
The level of musicianship, the originality and their ability to connect with their audience made them teen idols, at least anywhere west of Idaho. Their shows became legendary, inspiring a generation of Pacific Northwest rockers.
Seaside's Tom Horning described the atmosphere as "Gidget Goes Crazy."
Through the three years of the riots, his mother refused to let him and his older brother go downtown near the clubs.

Lester Raw, Seaside mayor from 1949-1960.

A CHANGE AT THE TOP

Maurice Pysher's introduction to Seaside politics was inauspicious, with a misspelling of his name in the local newspaper, the *Signal* reported.
There will be at least two candidates for mayor of Seaside on Election Day, Nov. 8, they wrote, incumbent Lester Raw and "Morris Pizer," a retired Portland plumbing company employee.

Pysher, described in the *Oregon Journal* as "a big white-haired man of 68," had lived in Portland most of his life where he was sales manager and heating engineer for Standard Supply Company.

In Seaside he purchased a six-unit apartment house in which he lived and managed in semi-retirement while still acting also as Standard's heating engineer. He made his bid for mayor in the fall of 1960.

Lester Raw contributed to Seaside throughout his life with a reputation "for honorable dealings, quiet determination and leadership,"

Lester Raw rose from being a hotel clerk in the 1930s to an owner of multiple businesses as well as a political and civic leader.

With his brother Vernon, Lester Raw entered the "saloon" business after the repeal of Prohibition. Gambling operations – slots, bingo and card games, then regulated by the city and not the state – flourished throughout the city.

Vern's Arcade became the first stop for kids and adults alike, offering pinball, Fascination, skee-ball and shooting galleries.

The Raws later successfully entered the hotel business, with ownership of the City Center and purchase of the former Seaside Hotel, a beachfront hotel at the northern corner of Broadway and the Turnaround – renaming it the "Seasider" and making it inviting enough for U.S. Senator John F. Kennedy to stay there in 1959 when he spoke to the national conference of the American Federation of Labor.

Vern Raw first took office as mayor in 1949 and served through the next decade. They were "in" with *Seaside Signal* publisher Max Schafer; members of the Chamber of Commerce and its adjunct, the Jaycees; and as downtown business owners, respected by their cohorts along the city's main streets.

Maurice Pysher – pronounced "Pie-sher"– an "outsider" from Portland who had lived in Seaside for a mere year and a half, did not like the cozy arrangements he saw around him.

The city was chokingly tight-knit, exclusionary and not as welcoming as he would have liked. Family values were being surrendered for the sake of the almighty dollar. He didn't like the rowdy kids who came down on weekends or the hotel owners who packed them into rooms, driving away more wholesome visitors.

And he didn't like the "old boy" network in Seaside that kept the system alive. He accused them of getting sweet deals on gambling and liquor revenues. He felt shut out. To Pysher and others, the Raws and their peers were everything that was wrong with Seaside.

Pysher didn't object to gambling, he said, but the way it worked in Seaside was skewed to the benefit of a few.

If it did continue, he would insist in his 1960 mayoral campaign, he sought "equal opportunities" for all who want to run such operations a thinly veiled attack on the Raws and their businesses.

He wanted to end Lester Raw's 12-year grip on City Hall. In September, he joined the race for mayor, appealing to voters to shake things up.

"This is the first time I ever ran for office," Pysher told the *Oregon Journal*. "Frankly, my only experience was some knowledge of parliamentary rules and running sales meetings and being a member of the Lions Club."

Decision day

Labor Day 1960 was relatively quiet in Seaside.

"There was no trouble on the beach or in the surf and damage and vandalism were at a minimum," reported the weekly *Signal*.

Nevertheless, eight weeks before the November election (the marquee contest: John F. Kennedy vs. Richard M. Nixon) Pysher saw a crisis.

Seaside's teen parties and drinking were hurting tourism, he said, and "tourists just quit coming."

He proposed "a concentrated drive to redeem the lost tourist goodwill and the vanished tourist dollars. ... It can be done."

In a "frank and honest" statement published days before the election, Pysher said if elected he would try to get a bill passed to limit future mayors to a single four-year term.

"This will eliminate the possibility of building up any powerful machine, using the power of mayor and political influence to further private advantages, or personal gain," Pysher said. "The time has come to think, to consider, to admit the known facts to do something for Seaside to stop pussy-footing and come out for the truth, fair play, and government by and for the people."

He wanted to dismantle what he perceived as Seaside's machine politics. After a dozen years of holding office, he asked, why was the present administration spending so much effort and money to hold this power longer?

Pysher announced he would decline campaign contributions because of strings attached that would tie him to a policy of favoritism. He pledged to institute "strict economy" and to bring the return of "sportsmen and tourists" while making "an effort to correct the teenage scandal."

He would work to run the city administration like a business, with "terrific savings" to taxpayers.

Lester Raw countered that there is "no easy road" for a public official. "He must be willing to follow the hard road, the road of right decisions made in the interest of those whom he has chosen to serve."

In a Seaside Chamber of Commerce forum, Raw pointed to his long tenure, city improvements to bridges, water and sewage, and the acquisition of highway funds for improvements. He highlighted the completion of the city airport, plans for retirement homes, and sustained yields in the local timber industry.

"Our tourist crowds are increasing and we have enjoyed our biggest convention year," Raw said. "Our future is surely bright."

He pointed to the need for renewed tourist promotion and said he had done "everything possible" toward that end.

Teens weren't the problem; they were an asset, Raw said. "Let's not run down all of our kids because of the 3 to 5 percent that cause all the trouble."

He returned jabs at his challenger and proclaimed his own knowledge and experience.

> "There are those who would seek public office believing that it is better to be clever than to be wise; that the labors of officials and employees have not been fruitful; that all is not well at City Hall; that certain elements are taking over our city. There is no substitute for experience and knowledge of city affairs."

His supporters agreed: the Raw brothers were fine men – sons of a Methodist minister – who made their money in Seaside and put it all back into Seaside.

The week before the election, *Signal* publisher Max Schafer endorsed Raw, defending him "rumors" circulating that are" nothing more than malicious gossip without any foundation in fact.

"Others are distortions of the truth, and entirely unfounded," the publisher wrote. "He (Raw) has done everything possible to make public every item of city business and no business has been transacted in private. And all of it has been reported."

Schafer and the *Signal* entered the Raws' corner, taking Pysher's lack of experience to task in a newspaper endorsement.

> "It is conceivable that a person with scant knowledge of the community, who has played no part in civic affairs, and who has taken no interest in city affairs, would make a successful mayor. But the odds are against it. We have always been of the opinion that an individual with ambitions to be mayor should first serve at least one term on the City Council. This would give him an opportunity to learn the complex process of maintaining a city government. At the

same time it would permit him to make a record so that voters would know what they are looking for."

He denied favoritism, deals or "finagling" of any kind by Raw, or by extension, his brother Vern.
Despite the *Signal*'s endorsement and Raw's long record as mayor, the incumbent was defeated at the polls.
Pysher received 54% of the 1,937 votes cast, defeating the multiterm mayor.
The election brought out the heaviest vote in any city election in the history of the city, with 1,934 people going to polls, out of 2,431 registered votes. Pysher won by large majorities in each of the city's six precincts.

Members of the Seaside City Council held the first meeting of 1961 January 9 in the city hall council chambers with a standing room only audience of citizens in attendance. The men are, standing, from left, B. E. Dennon, appointed to fill the vacancy left by Roy Hicks; Ervin Smith, V. Y. Davis, Connie Grabb, Emmett Brown and John Royce. Mayor Maurice Pysher is seated.

The *Signal* announced a change of administration in Seaside.

CHIEF'S FIRING LEADS TO BROUHAHA

The crowd at the Jan. 9, 1961, Seaside City Council meeting was so large it spilled out of City Hall and onto the street.

Newly elected Seaside Mayor Maurice Pysher opened the meeting by addressing the packed council chamber with a welcome and hope to have their cooperation to help Seaside go forward with the change they wanted.

His first dramatic action taking office was to fire the police chief.

The new council divided into pro-Smith – and by extension, supporters of the previous mayor, Lester Raw – and pro-Pysher factions.

Councilor Vernon Davis, a superintendent for the logging firm Crown Zellerbach, said he believed Smith was entitled to have the reason for his removal from office stated and the reasons made public.

Councilor Connie Grabb, aligning with Pysher, said the change in the police force had been a campaign promise.

The next chief appointed "should be depended upon to work with the mayor and council for the next administration," Pysher said.

Smith's supporters pushed back. Seasiders appreciated Smith's way of handling difficult problems and maintaining the peace.

He enforced the law fairly and without favor and did not deserve to be demoted, said former mayor William Hollenbeck, a meeting attendee.

A woman at the meeting asked why the mayor hadn't revealed his intentions to replace the chief during the November campaign.

Pysher sidestepped the issue.

He was there to "please the majority and would do so to the best of his ability."

"We want to make Seaside the most attractive resort in the Northwest and the only interest we have as to what is best for the majority," Pysher said. "We have no axe to grind, no business interests to foster, and no relatives to favor. With cooperation on the part of the people of Seaside the people of the Northwest will again flock to Seaside for the recreation."

Pysher said he would find Smith another city position – albeit at a salary substantially less than the police chief's $6,200 per year annual salary.

"I have no idea of doing anything that is not in the best interest of the majority of the people of Seaside," Pysher said. "I consider my election as a great honor and I'm well aware of the responsibility involved. The voters indicated that they wanted to change and we are expected to give them a change. This does not mean a change from bad to good but from fine to a little better."

With Smith's sudden dismissal, police officer Leonard Schaer and municipal judge Mo Swenson immediately resigned in solidarity.

John Yarmonchik, a longtime Seaside police officer, was named to take Smith's place. Yarmonchik, 39, a veteran of 11 years on the force, had been night sergeant for eight years. Smith was placed on vacation leave, leading Pysher to offer the ex-chief city employment in some other capacity.

Smith wasn't so quick to take a demotion.

"I might stay with the city," Smith said in response, "but not as a janitor."

In the course of the night Mayor Pysher asserted his power as mayor repeatedly. He used the gavel to call attendees "out of order," ordered a new city financial audit to unearth perceived irregularities, and handpicked a new city councilor, Bud Dennon, after the elected candidate, Roy Hicks, announced a move out of the city.

Discord becomes statewide issue

The *Signal* newspaper tended to boosterism at the period. But the *Oregonian* – the premier paper in the state – and the *Oregon Sunday Journal* both kept a close eye on the changes in Seaside's city hall administration.

The *Journal* was quick to pick up on the city's discord, and Pysher could feel more comfortable sharing his vision with them than the hostile *Signal*.

After the year's first council meeting, "the town is seething," *Journal* reporter Jim Running wrote, split between supporters of the new mayor and deposed Lester Raw. It was former police chief Smith's loyalty to former Mayor Lester Raw that motivated Pysher's decision to replace him.

"All during the campaign, Sid Smith used a city-owned car, city-purchased gasoline, full police chief regalia, and on city time deliberately went out and campaigned vigorously to keep me from being elected," he told the *Journal*. "After I was elected he never once got in touch with me as the newly elected mayor. Under these conditions, it would be impossible for me to trust this man's loyalty as my chief of police."

Pysher declared that Seaside was due for a change, "and in some cases, a radical change."

He intended to make Seaside "more courteous to visitors," he said, paradoxically calling Seaside "a resort town where people come to let their hair down and have fun."

"And now we'd like to have it advertised as under new management," Pysher said. "We want people to have good clean, fun and enjoy themselves and not wind up in jail doing so. We're definitely not going to make a Sunday School town out of it. On the other hand, we're not going to permit a bunch of stumbling drunks to come down and take over."

Pysher took up a theme from his 1960 mayoral campaign, telling the *Journal* he planned on cracking down on illegal gambling operations – including the nickel, dime, quarter and half-dollar slot machines in the Elks and Moose clubs.

The noisy attention for Seaside's controversial new administration from the big city newspaper drew a response from *Signal* editor Max Schafer in an editorial. He

resented Pysher bypassing his own newspaper fiefdom for the out-of-touch Portland press. He labeled the *Journal* piece as "decidedly untrue" and "extremely damaging" to Seaside.
"It presents a confused picture which cannot only mislead the uninformed reader, but must have led a lot of people to wonder if Seaside is a community of morons." The piece portrayed Seaside as a corrupt drunken gambling town, Schafer wrote.

> "The question of gambling was publicized in such a way as to infer that Seaside is more or less of an open town. There is as much gambling here as any small town. Almost any community in Oregon has private clubs, where members can have the dubious pleasure of yanking on the handle of a one-armed bandit. There are usually places where a card game is underway."

As for Pysher's charges of favoritism toward Lester Raw and his business enterprises, Schafer pointed out:

> "The city licenses pinball machines, as they've been declared illegal as amusement devices by the state Supreme Court. The city does not license slot machines. No operator has an exclusive franchise for coin-operated machines in Seaside. The field is open. It has always been open. In fact at least three operators have had machines in Seaside during the past few years."

Fallout

Sid Smith's dismissal hit a nerve. Here was the police chief who had kept their kids safe, presented a friendly face and developed a personal relationship with residents over his time in Seaside. Decades later, Seaside author Gloria Linkey still glowingly remembered Smith as a "wonderful man."
At a special meeting the next Monday, Jan. 16, angry residents in droves turned out to protest the firing of the former police chief. At its close, it ended with a shouting match.
City Hall was packed as Pysher laid out an organizational chart that portrayed his new vision for the city.

The chart indicated that he would personally supervise the city attorney, the water department, city engineer, building inspector, police, auditor and judge, with Pysher selecting George Cole out of four applicants for the position.

Dick Walter of the Jaycees – the Junior Chamber of Commerce – read a letter enumerating 10 charges against the new mayor and his conduct during the Jan. 9 council meeting.

Members were still seething over the events of that previous meeting. There had been no Pledge of Allegiance to the flag, no call for invocation and overall lack of knowledge of council procedure. The new mayor, they said, was clueless as to how to run a meeting according to Robert's Rules of Order.

Along with these procedural concerns, the Jaycees objected to what they described as a "suppression" of correspondence by the new mayor and council. Pysher and his allies had pre-selected Bud Dennon to fill the term of Roy Hicks before the open council meeting, they said, without public input.

"You declared that you want cooperation," a resident said pointedly to Pysher. "We have the right to cooperation too."

Pysher shifted blame to his council.

"I did not do all this," Pysher replied. "It was done by the council. Members of the council are better acquainted with the situation than I am."

There was nothing personal about Smith's dismissal, Pysher said. The decision was driven by Smith's cozy relationship with former Mayor Raw.

"If you were sitting as mayor and permitted personal friendship to influence you, I would consider that to be wrong," Pysher said. "It is a known fact that Smith and I could have never operated together in harness."

If you cannot trust a man's loyalty, he added, "your operation would break down."

Impugning Smith's loyalty was a bridge too far for the crowd that adored him.

At that point there was an "audible gasp from the crowded council chamber," the *Signal* reported, "with an overtone of astounded protest."

The accusations of improper conduct, without proof, infuriated many in the crowd, especially Raw's friends and supporters.

Council members should have given Smith a chance to answer charges in an open meeting, attendees said. Members of the council should have known enough to consult with constituents before making important changes in the police department.

The Smith affair was a star chamber proceeding – Smith had a right to face his accusers.

Smith's firing was necessary to refresh the city's image, Pysher responded. The voters wanted courtesy on the part of the police department. One way to get it is to make changes in the police force."

Connie Grabb, a member of the council aligned with the new mayor, inadvertently threw fuel to the fire when he said that the whole question of the police force had been discussed in a private meeting of the council.

Grabb, perhaps unaware of the state's open meetings laws, said that the decision had been made at an informal get-together of council members.

Dick Walter of the Jaycees was livid. He quoted the city charter to the effect that all meetings should be public.

Smith supporter Ken Anderson said he had no objection to any council action – provided it was done in a proper manner.

Anderson declared that there were few Seaside residents who had not seen Smith go beyond the requirements of duty.

A grievous wrong had been done, Anderson declared, and Smith was entitled to a fair hearing. He wanted to know what the council was going to make it up for Smith and his years of service.

Pysher and the councilors remained silent as Anderson repeated the question several times without a response.

Finally, seeking an end to the uncomfortable, deadlocked conversation and angry critics, demanded the audience "show some courtesy."

This only inflamed attendees, who demanded Pysher provide his definition of courtesy.

Pysher said it could easily be found in the dictionary, adding that the audience, not he, were the discourteous ones. It was not the business of the council to listen to a "debating society," he declared.

The meeting ended to no one's satisfaction.

The *Signal* would later report in a rare all-caps headline on page one: "COUNCIL MEET ERUPTS INTO BATTLE OVER SMITH; SOME WORK DONE."

A subhead noted: "Irregularities claimed in council meeting."

TABLE 6

ARRESTS OF MALES, ALL AGE GROUPS, BY YEAR, OFFENSE, AND HOLIDAY/NON-HOLIDAY, IN PERCENTS

Category of Offense	Non-Holiday Sample	Memorial Day	Independence Day	Labor Day
1960				
Liquor	33	44	64	72
Traffic	40	24	22	12
Conduct	13	26	4	14
Felony	3	-	-	-
All other	10	6	9	2
N	119	34	45	50
1961				
Liquor	41	48	63	69
Traffic	37	19	18	14
Conduct	16	33	9	15
Felony	1	-	-	-
All other	5	-	9	2
N	93	21	95	118

A state report analyzed crime statistics in Seaside in 1960 and 1961.

YOUTH CRACKDOWN

Seaside hoped to secure its reputation as a preferred tourist destination with publicity campaigns designed to attract families and adults.

With Baby Boomers reaching high school age, enrollment at Seaside High School for the 1961-62 school year was the largest ever. The school exceeded its capacity for the first time, with 403 students – three over the maximum of 400.

The Seaside Chamber of Commerce reported "excellent response" to its early 1962 tourist mailers.

Almost 1,000 Seaside travel discount coupons were carried in newspapers throughout the Northwest and in Western Canada and in one ad in the Pacific Coast edition of Sunset Magazine. The city spent $3,000 in newspaper advertising, $1,200 for TV spots and $250 for radio spots in an attempt to induce parents to accompany their children to Seaside, the weekly *Signal* reported. Anyone under 21, it was understood, was better off going elsewhere.

The Seaside Chamber of Commerce reported "excellent response" to its early 1962 tourist mailers. And despite the turmoil in city hall, the city had reason for optimism. Building permits for the year totaled $1.58 million, a record for Seaside, up from $378,000 the year before.

That spring the Seasider Hotel hosted conventions for the 150-delegate Oregon Coast Association, the annual convention of the International Association of Personnel in Employment Security, and the Society of American Foresters. Chevrolet employees came later in May, as members of the University of Oregon Dental School faculty.

The city had a grand vision for the future, inspired by the scenic beauty and affluence of vacation cities to the south like Palm Springs or Carmel, California.

Seaside editor Max Schafer viewed, the snazzy Northern California beach town outside of Monterey, as a model for Seaside's future. "We certainly admired the cleanliness and neatness of Carmel, and certainly think that Seaside can be improved by making it cleaner and neater than it is."

The business community's optimism was tempered with Pysher's obsession with cracking down on "misinformed youth in their attempts to take over the town." Retirees didn't want to remake Seaside into a Carmel, Palm Springs or anywhere else. They were instead focused on the perceived youth menace and its threat to their hopes of a peaceful retirement.

The new police chief shared Pysher's goals.

For both Independence Day and Labor Day holidays in 1961, police presence and response was ratcheted up. Arrests more than doubled in Chief Yarmonchik's first year of office.

Young people who had been in earlier years encouraged to come to Seaside now found themselves unwelcome, wrote Ken Polk in a 1965 state report, "The Seaside Riots," prepared for the Office of Juvenile Deliquency and Youth Development. According to his analysis, the new Seaside administration pressed an agenda of reigning in youth.

"In the context of the unprecedented strictness shown by the police toward youth during the previous year," wrote Polk, "the mayor's remarks amounted to a challenge to youth to go ahead and riot, because the city was ready and waiting."

'Youth lawlessness'
In the past, the city had provided "all the needs of a 'good time.'"
This meant housing, booze, gambling and "available women or men."
The mayor recommended that the council make an effort to change state legal protections for minors – referring to limits on police detainment, stiffer penalties and barriers to overnight rentals – laws which tied the hands of the city in dealing with law violators under 21.
Pysher declared that the city now had a police department controlled and supervised by the mayor himself and three councilors. The city attorney presented proposals for a change in juvenile enforcement, replacing lax ordinances that "prevent the progress or growth of the city."
These included higher fines for disorderly conduct, bans on hotel stays for minors, and a change to the length of time youths could be held in detention.
When two local juveniles were charged in a series of burglaries in Seaside and Gearhart, even the *Signal*, in a sign of cooperation with the new mayor – or recognizing a tide of public sentiment – joined the call for attention to the "mounting rate" of youth lawlessness.
"We are disturbed by the amount of juvenile crime," publisher Max Schafer wrote. "For many years there has been less trouble with juveniles here than in most communities in the past, all but it's been a minor nature. Recently vandalism, theft and burglary have occurred and these things have been done by local youths."
The city now enjoyed police protection "which combines friendly and courteous and efficient law enforcement."

The wrong direction
On March 8, 1962, the eve of spring vacation for the Portland schools, Chief Yarmonchik laid down the second major challenge to youth coming to Seaside, wrote the *Signal*.
"Yarmonchik says that he does not want to be tough on the youngsters but that he has no intention whatsoever of letting them get out of hand. The instructions to the police are to process every infraction of the law no matter how minor, in order to emphasize the fact that Seaside expects the visitors to be orderly. The theory is that once this is understood, there will be little trouble."

Seaside police added an extra policeman and night shifts so "that almost all of the Seaside police force will be on duty nights, when most of the difficulty with youngsters occurs."

The *Signal* struck a sympathetic note to teens, describing them as "for the most part orderly," but joined the mayor and police chief in decrying trouble originating from "older youngsters who follow the students to Seaside with nothing but trouble in mind."

Even before the March 1962 holiday week, three Portland teens were charged after driving their car onto the beach and using it for target practice, shooting it full of holes.

No one cared, the *Signal* reported, except for the fact that every time they hit a bump driving it back, glass dropped out of the shattered windows and onto the street. Over the break, police set a record number of arrests, charging 67 adults with crimes of disorderly conduct, drinking and reckless driving.

The editorials, police measures, Portland reporting and messaging from the top, along with the city's push for an older and more family-oriented crowd did little to deter — if it actually didn't help fuel — a 1962 spring break "invasion."

The week started quietly, but apparently the kids were lying in wait, the *Signal* reported.

They worked up a full head of steam as their vacation drew to a close, coming to Seaside's beaches for dancing, drinking and partying. Police logged one of the busiest vacations, with 67 arrests of young people between the ages of 18 and 21. An additional 20 to 25 minors were arrested on various charges before the police stopped counting.

To counter the trend, Pysher and the Chamber of Commerce sought to provide alternative, more positive activities for young people. The mayor proclaimed May 24 the start of "Clean-up, Plant-up and Paint-up Week," with the Junior Chamber of Commerce to paint the face of the Turnaround. Images of Tom Sawyers holding paintbrushes and white-washing fences were splashed over the front page of the *Signal*.

Perhaps it would be possible to rebound from the spring break rowdiness, to discourage and weed out the troublemakers and host what they hoped would be respectful, well-behaved model citizens.

Results from the July 4th weekend were unreliable; rainy weather kept attendance down and only a handful of arrests made.

Moving forward, the city focused on wholesome activities, like the Miss Oregon pageant, crab feeds and the 54th annual dahlia parade, sponsored by the fire department.

Seaside was optimistic going into Labor Day 1962, with a plan advanced for a Seaside "Indian Summer" program to be carried out after the holiday with promotions including a camera day, treasure hunt and kite-flying.

The events of Saturday, Sept. 1 and Sunday, Sept. 2 took almost everyone by surprise.

Kids enjoy soft drinks at the under-21 Pypo Club.

DRAGGING THE GUT

If music can be said to calm a riot, the Pypo Club in Seaside in 1962 would receive that designation.

The youth club – pronounced "pie-po," with the accent on the first syllable and named after a small, saucer-shaped skimboard – was the start of a trend, alcohol-free hangouts for teens 16-21 with dancing and bands.

Seaside High School graduate Joe Camberg hatched the idea for a teens-only nightclub in 1961.

Steve Johnson, Joe's football coach at Seaside signed on as the adult of the trio with the valued assistance of Oney Camberg, Joe's mother.

The Pypo Club opened in the summer of 1961 at No. 1 Broadway – the Turnaround Building – which also housed the indoor heated saltwater natatorium. The club filled the space vacated by the American Legion, which moved to new digs on the east side of the highway.

They charged 25 cents admission – later 50 cents – and breath-tested each teen for traces of alcohol, Seaside's Leah Griffith remembered. Drinks like "Seafoam

Slurpers" and "Pypo Punches" for a quarter, with straight drinks 15 cents.

The club was the product of "Oney" Lenora (Kelly) Normand Camberg, born in Astoria, Oregon on July 23, 1908, a woman the local historian Helen Gaston called "a legend in her own time."

Oney operated a bar on the Sunset Highway outside of Seaside, and word had it that she was tough enough to throw the loggers out of her bar when they became unruly. "Any of the other loggers would have helped her if she needed it," Gaston said in a 1993 remembrance. "She was known as a fun-loving, but strict proprietor."

When her husband Art Normand died of a heart attack in 1938, with only a small income from the post office, store, and the school bus job, Oney had to do something else to support her family. On June 18, 1938, she opened "Oney's" as a beer parlor. She married Albert "Bud" Camberg in 1940, and they had a son, Joe, born three years later.

Wrote Gaston:

> "On July 4, 1952, Bud was hit by a car as he walked along the highway out at Elsie. He was severely injured and was never able to work again as a logger. He did learn to do the books for the business and helped in that way, but Oney again had the responsibility of being the family provider.
>
> "When it was time for Joe to go to high school, in 1959, Oney decided to transfer him to Seaside so he could play football and be involved with other sports. She bought a house on the Prom in Seaside so he would have a place to take his friends. She was always supportive of his athletic achievements and attended almost every game. She became a second mom and friend to the whole team."

In 1962, Oney decided to put Joe to work, "so he wouldn't be a bum." She leased a little restaurant on Broadway in Seaside and called it Little Oney's. It was Joe's first business venture.

That same year, Joe, Seaside High School teacher Steve Johnson and lifeguard Gil Tolan decided they wanted to open a teen center. With Oney's help they rented the old American Legion Club above the natatorium – an indoor community swimming pool at the Broadway Turnaround – and started the Pypo Club.

Jim Roehm, whose family owned Roehm's Furniture on Broadway and Holladay, was a Seaside grad attending Oregon State University. He was in Seaside in the summer of 1962 working for the logging company, Crown Zellerbach.

He remembered Oney for her prodigious weight – about 300 pounds at a height of 5'6" tall. Along with the Pypo Club and her other eateries on the highway, she opened a small restaurant on Broadway called "Little Oney's."

Hotrodders would "drag the gut," Roehm said.

"Typically on a Saturday, every weekend, you would have cars packed going up Broadway," Roehm said. "I mean, it was a real car culture back then. You went around the Turnaround, came back down to Columbia, turned south, went down to Downing Street and got back in line and drove up again. There were guys in my high school that that was their whole life, customizing their cars. That's how they showed them off. It would take a half-hour to get from Downing Street to the Turnaround.

"On weekends, Labor Day, it would be packed," he continued. "You could hardly walk on the streets because there were so many people."

Jeanne Nordmark, 18 in 1962, remembered Oney as a "really nice lady."

"You didn't mess around with her," Nordmark said. "She was a tough cookie. If we went to order something and then we said, 'Oh, we changed our mind,' you'd get that order anyway.

"She always treated us real good," Nordmark added. "She took a real interest. But when she came into town, well, she didn't mess around. At all."

Oney owned a home on the South Prom, Gil Tolan's younger brother Tod recalled. Joe Camberg and Gil Tolan were both students at Oregon State University. Tolan worked at the Crab Broiler restaurant and Camberg ran a tiny burger bar on Broadway.

"One night after work Joe and Gil stopped by our house with this crazy idea of a 'teenage night club.' I figured they were nuts," Tod Tolan said. "Because they were both minors, they enlisted the Seaside football coach, Steve Johnson, into the trio."

The group went before the City Council with an application for a "teenage restaurant for dancing and serving of soft drinks and sandwiches" at Seaside's Turnaround. Johnson would be in charge and proper supervision would be provided.

According to Helen Gaston:

> "They hired football players and the coach Steve Johnson as security. It was strictly for youth, 14 to 20 years old. They opened at 8:30 p.m. and closed at 11. The parents could come in and watch for a short time, but they couldn't stay. ... Oney was always around. The kids liked and respected her though she was a strict disciplinarian."

James Manolides, a member of the Pacific Northwest rock band James Henry and the Olympics, wrote in 2011 that the city felt it would be good if the kids had a place to meet, dance and have a soda to "keep them off the streets."
John Spence, who worked as a lifeguard in Seaside while a student at the University of Washington, was doing beach duty with three other young men – Tolan, Roy "Hodun" Parnell and Dick "Kahuna" Rankin in the summer of 1962.
 a small attic room in an old boarding house when he met Steve Johnson, the Seaside football coach and in charge of security at the Pypo Club.
Johnson invited him to move into more spacious quarters in Gearhart, and Spence joined Johnson and his roommate, Jim Ryder, a Seaside track coach.
"They're four or five years older than me and knew everything and knew everybody," Spence said. "I'm this average kid brought into this incredible beach scene. Not only did they help my self-confidence, but being head lifeguard was the first time I had any responsibility. It just felt real natural."
Another lifeguard fondly dubbed Spence "Moondoggie," after the character in "Gidget" and its sequels who saves – and later woos – Gidget.
"I had black hair and looked like James Darren, the actor," Spence said. "Folks started calling us 'salt and pepper' – the blonde white guy and his dark-skinned, black-haired sidekick."
Spence met his first wife – Miss Seaside 1960 Dyann Van Sickle – while here.
Seaside's Ky Weed Jennings knew Steve Johnson well as her journalism and psychology teacher in her junior and senior years of high school, and later as a friend. Weed worked at the club during the first year it opened, along with Johnson, Joe Camberg and Gil Tolan, an Oregon State University student who spent summers in Seaside.
"Steve said, 'Ky, you're going to be behind the bar!'" she recalled.

It may have been more than a little bit like the set of a '60s beach movie in rock 'n' roll Seaside, where young people danced to Paul Revere and the Raiders, the Kingsmen, the Wailers and other Pacific Northwest bands.

The club was so successful that other communities saw it as a model.

The Pypo Club became an immediate success and gained attention from cities in Oregon and Washington.

When a Portland youth commission considered a teenage recreation hall project, Johnson was asked to travel to Portland and speak at a special meeting, the *Signal* reported.

"Meeting with the Multnomah County Youth Commission has caused me to more fully appreciate the cooperation the City Council and Seaside police force have given the Pypo Club," Johnson said in May 1962. "I advised the youth commission to consider setting up an establishment similar to the Pypo Club only if they could find an individual who knew young people well and who would be willing to devote a great deal of time to seeing the project through to a successful beginning. Our attitude of fulfilling a need rather than providing a service has gained us the approval of our customers."

'Louie Louie'

The Northwest scene was legendary, and at times even met or eclipsed the rock 'n' roll sound from England, wrote author Dave Marsh, in *Louie Louie: The History and Mythology of the World's Most Famous Rock 'n' Roll Song*.

> "The teenage rock bands of the Pacific Northwest built a great lost rock 'n' roll scene in those years when the Big Beat wandered in the wilderness and not only that, without the help of a single Brit, created one of the first great modern rock scenes, one in which spirit and community were central for both musicians and audiences."

Tacoma's Lawrence Fewell Roberts II – nicknamed "Rockin' Robin" after the No. 1 hit by Bobby Day – was known for his boundless energy. Still a high schooler, he joined the Tacoma, Washington-based rhythm and blues band, the Blue Notes, in 1957.

In his history of Pacific Northwest rock 'n' roll, *Sonic Boom: The History of Northwest Rock, from Louie Louie to Smells Like Teen Spirit,* author Peter Blecha called the Blue Notes "the original DIY band."

"Their efforts to polish their own version of an R&B stage show not only won them fans amongst their own age group, but made them Tacoma's hottest musical property."

In 1959, Roberts joined another Tacoma, Washington, band, "The Wailers," who had mainly been known for their role in helping define the original Pacific Northwest rock sound.

The addition of Roberts proved to be a wise move: Roberts's energetic manner, riveting voice, and deep knowledge of R&B music all combined to make him a charismatic front man. The band formed its own record company, Etiquette Records, an unprecedented move for a teenaged group.

"They would soon upstage the Blue Notes and then go on to challenge the top Seattle bands as well," wrote Blecha.

Roberts established a reputation as a high-voltage rockin' R&B singer who worked the stage with wild abandon.

As Buck Ormsby, the Wailers' electric bass player, soon realized:

"He was one of the ... best singers I ever heard," Ormsby said. "He was an ad-libber. He could take any song and turn it into his own song. And he was talented enough to get that energy going with everybody. He was real high-strung – always a volcano ready to go. Real dynamic and entertaining on stage."

The Wailers rode the "Louie Louie" wave in 1961, with the first "garage band" version of the song.

Based on the 1956 single by Los Angeles-based Richard Berry and the Pharaohs, Roberts introduced locals to the song at weekend teen dances.

The Wailers had a regional hit with "Louie Louie," but that was soon eclipsed by the version by the Kingsmen, a Portland-based group familiar to the Seaside scene. Blecha quotes the Kingsmen's Jack Ely on his discovery of the song in Seaside. According to Ely:

> "We'd played the Pypo Club on a Saturday night and then went back there on set Sunday afternoon to pack up our gear. While we were in there 15 or 20 teenagers were hanging out and somebody

put the song 'Louie Louie' on the jukebox. And when it came on the jukebox, everybody in the room got up and started dancing. I mean everybody. They didn't even care whether they even had a partner. They just got up and stood around their tables and started dancing. And I didn't think too much about it."

As soon as the record ended, somebody would put the song on again – and again. "Somebody had plugged that jukebox so would play the same song over and over every time and every time," Ely recalled.
Ely turned to band members and declared, "We've got to learn this song."
A year later Seaside High School grad, Jerry Dennon, produced "Louie Louie" for the Kingsmen, who made it an iconic recording, its garbled, mysterious lyrics providing fodder for generations of rock 'n' roll sleuths.
There was no band scheduled at the Pypo Club that Labor Day, 1962, but Robin Roberts and Wailers were booked down the street, at the Bungalow, the cavernous dance hall on Broadway that had hosted bands from the 1920s on.
On Sept. 1, 1962, teenagers hopped into their cars from Oregon, Washington and Idaho and piled into hotels, motels, cabins and tents for their annual tribute to the end of summer.
In Seaside, the stage was set for Labor Day 1962.
Somehow, the Pypo Club, and that echoing lyric with its throbbing beat, would act as the stage for one of the wildest nights on the Oregon Coast.

Law enforcement used fire hoses to disperse crowds in the 1962 riots.

RIOT DAY ONE

What started Seaside's Labor Day riots?

Some say it was a rivalry between schools. Others attributed the start of the 1962 riot to ongoing clashes between bikers and car clubs. It could have been a fight over a girl. Some who lived it say that it was an ongoing dispute between Seaside lifeguards and out-of-town youth.

An easy availability of alcohol, a defiant attitude toward youth from local and business groups known as the "city fathers" — or it could have just been the weather.

"It's still my belief that it was pre-planned by a small group of older bored drunken guys who decided to raise havoc in Seaside that final summer weekend," Seaside's Ky Weed Jennings said. "And it became a clash with authority. What started out to be a normal Labor Day weekend of teenagers and college kids became a riot."

The resort city was "jammed with thousands of visitors," the *Oregonian* reported. There were so many vacationers "you couldn't get anybody else in without a shoe horn."

The weather was "really hot, very unusual – two or three days of 75 or 80 degrees down here," said Seaside's Dallas Cook.

High schools and colleges all were starting back the following week, Cook recalled. "Seaside was packed, particularly with college kids."

"You had lots of beer and whatever," Cook said. "Seaside police were – I wouldn't say they were nonexistent – but they were damn close to it. One thing led to another. It seems to me it was late afternoon that everything really cranked up."

Downtown was always full of teenagers from all over, Jennings said, and crowds at Labor Day were nothing new.

"Portland kids who came often and local kids, and they all got along with each other," she said. "They just rode around the Turnaround in cool cars with radios blaring, guys watching the girls, girls watching the guys, teenagers walking on sidewalks and hanging out."

Jennings can't pinpoint a specific incident that sparked the first night.

"I don't think there was just one," she said. "I think it was pre-planned by a group of men who were older who used to hang out in bars in Seaside. They were workers, not students, from Tacoma is what I always heard."

"The riot was not started by local kids," she said. "They got involved just from 'being there' but they did not instigate the riot."

A state report delivered two weeks later said the problem started in the morning as "a milling mob of youth with nothing to do" roamed up and down Broadway.

"Tension built up all day," the *Signal* reported. "Many (youths) were drinking heavily, some were looking for action, others were there to see the show."

Groups of kids began to get unruly about 5 p.m.; it appeared to be more rowdy and difficult crowd than usual. Fights started; two police tried to intervene and they were ignored. Others joined in and more gathered.

The crowd – estimated at 2,500 – milled downtown, singing and looking for something to do, wrote Warne Nunn, Governor Mark Hatfield's assistant, in a riot timeline.

At about 6:30 p.m., a new brawl erupted.

"Some guy in a car was yakking to somebody on the Prom," Cook said. "The guys in the car got the holy crap kicked out of them. The guy walked over to the Prom and beat the crap out of him. Right up there at the Turnaround the fuse was lit. It was 'Fight! Fight! Fight!'"

David Craig, writing in the Clatsop County Historical Society Quarterly in 2017, interviewed musician Stew Dodge.

Dodge, a senior at North Catholic High School in Portland in 1962, told Craig he and others were walking near the Times Theatre about a block from the beach when a fight broke out between two students.

"It was like a John Wayne movie," Dodge said. "These guys were slugging it out. It was a fair fight, but it was a real fight. Everybody backed up so there was like a 20-foot diameter ring right in the middle of the intersection where these guys were fighting.

"Everybody's cheering them on and finally they said, 'Do you want to quit?' 'Yeah I'll quit.' And they shook hands and walked down the street to get a beer and then the cops showed up."

One of the combatants was arrested, Dodge said, and put into a squad car.

The crowd followed them. "They tried to take a right hand turn at the Turnaround and they couldn't move," Dodge said.

> "It was really packed and people were yelling, screaming and cheering and stuff and drunk, everybody's drunk ... Somebody ran up and opened the passenger side, back door on the cop car and they grabbed the guy that was in the cop car and spirited him away."

Suddenly they didn't have their prisoner anymore — he slipped out the back seat of the police car and into the crowd. The police headed back into town and when they got in front of the Our Lady of Victory Catholic Church a block down the street, they found themselves blocked in.

From up the street toward the beach came a Blitz Weinhard stubby bottle through the air, punching out the rear window of the police car.

"And that was it," Dodge recalled.

'I think we have control'

Local radio deejays, getting word of the excitement, breathlessly announced the impending riot in Seaside. Local kids from Astoria, Warrenton, Cannon Beach and neighboring Gearhart headed downtown.

Jeanne Nordmark was one of those drawn to the scene by radio reports earlier in the evening. Then 18, she was living in nearby Warrenton. She told her mother – unaware of the activity 10 miles to the south – she was meeting a friend. They promptly headed toward the action.

"It was just a mass of kids suddenly going up to the Turnaround to see what was going on," Dallas Cook said. "Traffic didn't move. That's when it really started getting ugly. Everybody was pitching the cops shit."

George Nelson, 18 at the time, found safety atop the roof of the Seasider Hotel. He witnessed a crowd of college kids on the right side of the Turnaround, elbow-to-elbow, watching a fight in the middle.

Two Seaside police officers tried to pull them apart, Nelson said. "But they got thrown off, because these were pretty big kids. The crowd kind of looked at each other and said, 'You know, I think we have control.' That, to me, is when the whole thing began."

According to the *Signal*:

> "The whole affair had a carnival atmosphere and the hundreds of persons who milled around watching the excitement seemed to have no real understanding of what was happening. They cheered the rioters and booed the police. They interfered with the police whenever possible without actually participating in the melee."

Not only young males were in the fray. It is quite likely that without the encouragement of this "cheering section" the participants would have dispersed long before they did, the *Signal* opined.

Many of those in the cheering section were "young girls," the newspaper added.

It was nearly 7 p.m., however, before the Seaside police force became convinced that the situation was getting out of hand, wrote the *Signal*. "By the time they were fully aware of the trouble, it was too late to do much about it."

Bringing out the hoses

Mark Hansen was 16, just back from a summer job spraying crops in Eastern Oregon.

He remembers "guys on the rooftops throwing stuff around."

Beer bottles filled with sand flew like missiles.

"Friends of mine were doing crazy stuff," Hansen said. "I remember guys saying, 'We're going to get some chains and knock out the power!'"

"It was just anarchy," Stew Dodge said. "It was thousands of kids, with nobody in charge; everybody was drunk, having a great time."

Then began the chants of "Let's get the tower."

At 8:30, the crowd lifted the lifeguard tower on the beach, surging forward and lifting the lifeguard stand over the steps and concrete railings up from the beach. About 50 people picked it up, Dodge said, and stood it up in the middle of the Turnaround.

The crowd succeeded in lifting the tower over the stone wall to the Promenade, Dallas Cook said.

Rocks flew through windows of the Ford Electric Company; kids scrambling to get inside received cuts so severe they required hospital visits.

Cheryl Adamscheck, 16 at the time, worked in Vern's Arcade serving cotton candy, popcorn and soda, at the building that now houses Funland, also an arcade.

There were glass windows on the Broadway and Columbia street sides, right next to the snack bar at the door's entrance, Adamscheck said.

"I was behind glass on two sides," Adamscheck said. "What I remember is rocks being thrown towards me and being terrified that they were going to break the glass because they were coming so close. I only had one little corner where there was a wall, so I stood there and watched. I'll never forget it because I'd never seen anything like that in my life before."

The violence continued as Seaside police awaited reinforcement from the state, the sheriff and neighboring communities. In some cases, their arrival stirred more violence.

"A big guy threw a manhole cover at the cops," Cook said. "How much does a manhole cover weigh, 75, 80 pounds? The guy had to be 6-foot-6."

Tower on the move

State policeman Harold Leonhardt was the first state policeman to arrive on the scene, at about 6 p.m. Leonhardt, along with three other policemen, would be hospitalized with injuries.

Around 8 p.m., Clatsop County Sheriff Carl Bondietti arrived with about 20 steel-helmeted officers — the metal protection better to repel flying rocks and bottles thrown like bombs.

"Police would kind of push the crowd back towards the ocean," George Nelson said. "And then the crowd would start inching their way forward. This went back and forth for quite a while. And it got a little bit violent."

One person waving a 3-foot-square iron frame over his head charged the police but restrained before injuring anyone, the *Oregon Journal* reported.

"They're pushing us towards the beach and they're cracking heads," Hansen said.

Doug Barker remembers a police officer holding a woman in a headlock.

"Don't they ever feed you guys?" quipped one of the kids.

That quip was to cost him. Without losing his grip on the woman, the officer cracked the young man across the back of his legs with his baton, Barker said.

The audience leaving the Times Theatre after the showing of *The Spiral Road*, starring Rock Hudson and Burl Ives, a tear-jerker about a Dutch physician who treats leprosy, was met by the real-life mob scene on Broadway.

"Nobody in there was the wiser," Cook said. "All of a sudden, the doors open and here come all these people that have been in the theater. There were two big cops standing right there. And I remember one of them ax-handled the guy coming out of the theater right over the top of the head."

Nearby, at Leonard's Taffy, "they hit some guy" hard enough to send him through the window.

"They weren't nice at that point," Cook said.

Everyone, rioter, passerby or onlooker, was vulnerable.

"I was standing next to a mother and her 12-year-old daughter," George Nelson said. "These guys were serious."

When they said "go home," anyone who didn't was liable to get a blow from their stick, George Nelson said. "They tried to aim right for their shoulder right next to the neck and that pretty much knocked them out. These guys were serious."

Nelson saw a 12-year-old girl and her mother getting knocked out, "laid out flat on the ground."

Jim Roehm, a 21-year-old Oregon State University student, was walking downtown with his girlfriend when he was surprised to see Broadway blocked off.

"The first thing we saw, which was really weird, was that they had blocked off Broadway at Columbia at the Times Theatre, with sandwich boards that said 'CLOSED,'" Roehm said.

As he and his girlfriend headed to the beach, he saw the lifeguard tower on the move. Normally it was 50 yards down toward the ocean, he remembered. Now it was on the Turnaround.

"Something was wrong," Roehm said. "There were tons of college-age boys. It was pretty obvious there was a lot of testosterone flowing.

They were three sheets to the wind, drunk. I've never seen that many college kids together."

Roehm watched as they carried the tower down the street, hitting power and telephone lines stretched across Broadway before it fell, breaking one inebriated rioter's leg.

"There were some hurt rioters," Roehm said. "That was literally the first thing that happened within the first 10 minutes that I was up there."

Firefighters arrived at about 10:15 p.m., turning hydrant hoses on the crowd.

Dallas Cook remembers "women and little girls screaming" as they were sent in a flood toward the beach.

"The fire department – I mean, these guys don't want to be there in the first place – they back off and kids get the hoses," Cook said.

"And then they were turning the hoses on the cops, on the fire department, and everybody else. It just kind of went to hell in a handbasket from that point."

Jeanne Nordmark, drawn by the radio coverage with her friend, got caught in the gushing torrents and sent back out to the beach.

While some of those hosed found it to be all part of the "fun," others were hurt as they were swept onto the pavement or into buildings.

The indiscriminate water cannons led to a counter-assault on the authorities. Fire hoses were slashed and rendered useless, bricks, stones, and chunks of wood were thrown at police.

Curt Sagner was a volunteer fireman called out in the disturbance, his son, also named Curt, remembered. "They turned fire hoses on the kids because they had to do something,"

Sagner said. "They couldn't use weapons, so they did whatever they could."

Roehm said the hoses did little to deter the crowd surge.

"It wasn't getting anything done," Roehm said. "The guys that were up there rioting were enjoying it."

Roehm recalls the crowd lifting up one of the benches on the Turnaround.

"I mean a big bench – like 15 feet long," Roehm said.

Firefighters found themselves in the center of the fray.

Mike Manion, 26, a beefy 6-foot-4 – found himself pursued by the kids with the bench, Roehm said. "You can see they were going to get Manion with it. About then Manion has dropped the hose and is fighting for his life in a fistfight with some of these guys. And he gets hit on the head with one of these beer cans."

The blow sent him to the hospital for treatment.

The crowd, soaking wet, high on adrenaline and most likely stewed to the gills, with new energy seized a concrete bench from the Prom and lifted it on their shoulders. Their destination: the Trail's End Tavern for more beer.

"There are probably 20 guys holding this little bench and they're going to take it through the door," Roehm said.

From Little Oney's next door, Oney Camberg made her presence known in a formidable manner.

"Oney saw this happening and grabbed this big spoon used to make chili," Roehm continued. "Oney Camberg was, like, 300 pounds. She's huge, and only about five-foot-six. She was a large person and she walked out there with that spoon and walked in front of the door and challenged these guys. 'Go ahead. See how far you get.'"

'As far as you go'

As police from other jurisdictions arrived, the balance of power began to shift. State police advanced up the street swinging their clubs, the *Signal* reported at the time. Anyone who did not move when ordered to do so "was clobbered" and the Seaside police came along with a car to carry the victim to the jail.

Seaside's Doug Barker, then a teen, got clocked by an officer with a billy club, he recalled. "The officer said, 'This is as far as you go.' He wasn't aggressive at all, but the thing hit me in the chest."

One youngster caught "the business end of a club" from a trooper, wrote the *Signal*, crying, with blood running down his face.

When another officer came to lead him to the paddy wagon, "the youngster wailed that he 'wasn't doing nothing,'" wrote the *Signal*.

"What did you do when they told you to move?" the second officer asked.
"I said, 'Yessir!'"
"That's where you made your mistake," said the cop. "You should have moved."
The state police riot squad – a "kind of platoon," according to George Nelson, advanced up Broadway carrying hazel wood handles" – 36-inch hickory sticks with axes mounted, normally used for heavy clearing.
Those arrested were taken away by school buses and paddy wagons.
Police all had batons, Roehm said. "They had blackjacks. They went into a wedge formation and started down the street."
Suddenly, the riot came to an end as police moved into formation. "The crowd just busted apart," Roehm said.
State police superintendent H.G. "Fod" Maison and Warne Nunn – assistant to Governor Hatfield – arrived at midnight.
Firefighter Hugh McKenna later wrote:

> "Clear the street they did, in the most handsome fashion. When those 32 state troopers marched up the street, not one single rioter was left on his feet. They had most formidable looking clubs or batons, which they used skillfully and in a most admirable fashion."

At one a.m., the riot had "simmered down," wrote the *Oregonian*, though pockets of people continued to throw rocks and bottles at police.
At least eight people were hospitalized that day, including state policemen Henry Balensifer, John Ritter, Dan Primus and Harold Ritter and Seasider firefighter Manion.
The 70 arrested that day were herded into four small cells in the city jail, located on Broadway near Roosevelt Drive, adjacent to City Hall.
A 24-hour state police detachment was scheduled to stay in Seaside to prevent any further disturbance during the weekend, the *Oregonian* reported.
"There had been some drinking and the ringleaders appear to be college kids," Chief Yarmonchik told the *Oregonian*. "We face this problem every year with back-to-school kids."
This year, he added with some understatement, "it was a little wilder than usual."

While Saturday's violence was quelled, the unrest on Labor Day 1962 in Seaside was far from over. It would take some quick thinking and a controversial deal to avert even greater mayhem the next day.

The Wailers entertain the crowd from the roof of the Pypo Club in 1962.

How rock 'n' roll quelled a riot

Club-swinging police and a crowd of 500 people "clashed on the main street of this coastal resort city Sunday in the aftermath of Saturday night rioting that resulted in more than 60 arrests," AP reported Sunday morning.
One Seaside volunteer firefighter, Hugh McKenna, became famous overnight after collaring a young man nearly twice his size. The image was captured by *Oregonian* staff photographer Chuck von Wald and reprinted in newspapers around the world. The riots were suddenly an international story.
Windows of shops along Seaside's main street, Broadway, had been broken in the previous night's rioting, "signs pulled up, cars dented and car windows broken by debris."

Young people punctured tires of a county sheriff's car and slashed the seats. An indeterminate amount of fire hose was damaged or destroyed.

In a proclamation, Governor Hatfield announced an emergency situation in Seaside, "because of a serious disturbance of the peace or riot there or imminent danger thereof."

In consultation with the Police Superintendent Maison and National Guard adjutant Governor General Paul Kliever, Hatfield issued a proclamation calling on the public to refrain from violence, "other disturbance and all threats thereof."

An eight-man emergency squad trained specifically for riots from the Salem state police patrol headquarters, joined contingents from McMinnville, Milwaukie, Newport and Astoria.

Hatfield ordered state police, the National Guard and others to assist and cooperate with the mayor and Seaside's city authorities "until the emergency is over."

The governor suspended the sale of alcohol along the coast until Tuesday morning after the holiday, from Warrenton to the north and Arch Cape to the south, the tiny oceanfront community beyond Cannon Beach.

A 24-hour state police detachment remained in Seaside to prevent any further disturbance during the weekend, the *Oregonian* reported.

Stationed at the ferry landing in Astoria and south of Seaside, police checked suspicious-looking cars in the hopes of averting further trouble. Out-of-state teenagers were told to go home.

Thirty more people were picked up and charged in Seaside from midnight to 8 a.m. on Sunday morning, with charges of after-hour curfew violations, disorderly conduct, rioting, disobeying an officer, drunkenness, and one arrest for driving with four people in the front seat.

The jails in Seaside were so crowded that many were transported by school bus or Crown Zellerbach logging company crew bus to Astoria for holding.

Overnight arrestees included young men from Seattle, Olympia, Tacoma and Mercer Island, Washington; Oregonians from Tillamook, Portland, Eugene and Albany; and one person from Okaloosa, Florida.

Three minors were held in custody.

To avoid the after-hours curfew, youths who had managed to elude police sought refuge outside of the city's borders in neighboring Gearhart to the north, and

Cannon Beach to the south. They slept on the beach, in parked cars and along the road.

Musician Stew Dodge recounted in the *Oregon Historic Quarterly*:

> "Three or four of us walked out of town to Gearhart, which is the next town north, and we all slept in a barn. I don't know whose barn it was. It was Labor Day. It got pretty chilly that night but I can remember all of us slept in the hay in the corner of this barn because all of the highways were closed."

Craig Weston, whose family lived across from the Gearhart Golf Club, remembers teens in tents camped on the greens.

With an influx of law enforcement, dozens of young people in jails and most businesses shut, an uneasy tension hung over downtown Seaside on Sunday. Police and firemen on duty gradually relaxed, the *Astorian* wrote, but the shops – save a shooting gallery and a couple of restaurants – were closed.

The big Labor Day weekend business "was a bust," with bars and packaged liquor stores shut tight.

The Seasider Hotel, the *Oregonian* wrote, reported a loss of more than $5,000 and the popular restaurant the Crab Broiler suffered losses of $1,200 and the Par-Tee Room, the white-napkin restaurant by the golf course on the south end of town, lost $500 in business.

A blend of fear and astonishment reflected from the eyes of business operators and longtime residents of the resort town, wrote the *Astorian*.

"I've never seen anything like it," a hotel operator commented. "It scares the daylights out of you when you see a bunch of kids who probably are good ones when by themselves or in small groups, turned into a pack of animals at the drop of a hat."

Locked tight

On Sunday, following reports that some of the Seaside crowd planned to storm the jail in an effort to free those being held, the National Guardsman joined 70 state policemen in an attempt to preserve order for the rest of the holiday weekend, the *Statesman* reported.

National Guard troops ordered to the scene a few hours earlier watched from stations atop downtown buildings as police drove the crowd off the street and onto the beach. Other businesses up and down Broadway were locked tight.

Trim-looking National Guardsmen walked slowly back and forth overlooking the beach holding tear gas canisters in hand, described as "ready to use them at a moment's notice."

Rumors persisted all day of student reprisals and state police turned back out of state cars carrying college-age youths at several places on highways leading into town. Seaside police urged young people to leave town.

State police carrying billy clubs maintained the street patrol and police cars patrolled the downtown area. Young people lingered and watched. The presence of the National Guard led local businesspeople to believe a recurrence of the previous day's violence was anticipated.

Mayor Maurice Pysher had no doubts. He told UPI that the crowd of young people milling on the beach "were definitely planning to take over the town."

Pysher described the affair as "an absolute disgrace to the area. These young people are no good, a detriment to the community and a disgrace to themselves."

Pysher told the press the entire incident was an "outside, preplanned attempt to imitate riotous conduct at Fort Lauderdale, Florida, in recent years."

The mayor added: "It's the most disgraceful thing that's happened to us here. We've tried to care for our tourists and visitors in a courteous manner."

Tensions mount

In Seaside, Sunday afternoon's tension came to a head when more than 30 "shouting state policemen carrying baseball bats and axe handles" charged the hundreds of youths on the west end of Broadway and drove them to the beach, wrote the *Astorian*.

Guardsmen took up positions on rooftops as state troopers stood ready with tear gas canisters.

Sunday's crowd was controlled by a heavy law-enforcement presence and a concert on the beach.

An ugly situation loomed soon after 5 p.m., the *Oregonian* reported, when several 100 young people massed at the west end of Broadway, and apparently prepared to launch a second assault on the downtown area similar to the one on Saturday night.

National Guardsmen took up positions on rooftops along Broadway and white-helmeted state troopers advanced in formation — what Seaside's Mark Hansen called "a blue line of axe handles."

After a relatively quiet day, with all of the bars closed, several hundred youths swarmed from the beach onto the Turnaround and started to move down the street. This time, there were no fire hoses. Police used clubs to control the crowd.

"They're cracking heads — 'You get out of the way,'" Hansen recalled. "If somebody started mouthing off, they said, 'You guys are going to the beach.'"

Police herded hundreds of young people away from downtown and onto the sand. A few feet away a cordon of white-helmeted state police paced methodically around the Turnaround overlooking the beach.

As dusk approached, the students appeared restless, burning benches and furniture taken from the street. Leaders worried about a second attempt to storm the town, the *Oregonian* wrote.

> "What combination of human nature blended with mass psychology turns a good-time Oregon town into a town of near empty streets and locked buildings where the tension is so thick you can nearly taste it? Seaside was just such a tension-spiked town Sunday night after state police took axe handles to hand and convinced 1,500 or so persons that they were through fooling around the rioters mumbling and snarling like hunt animals huddled en masse on the beach thinking what they would like to do in wondering what their next move would be."

Music or mayhem?

The Wailers were booked at the roller rink on Broadway a block east of the Turnaround. But that concert had been canceled and the band was passing time in their second-story hotel room where they viewed the chaos.

Joe Camberg, manager of the Pypo Club, suggested that the Wailers be hired to play for a dance on the beach. Others in the crowd, including a New York serviceman identified as Don De Rigo, approached officials.

"'Can't one of you men get up on that public address system and talk some sense into those kids' heads?' pleaded a woman who in the crowd. 'They're good kids and something went wrong and they're acting like a bunch of thugs. I've got kids just like that them and they just want to go to do something.'"

A deputation of Camberg and others, with the agreement of the Wailers, negotiated the possibility with State Police Superintendent Maison, who gave his approval provided they limited dancing to the beach area.

Maison, with the support of the governor's assistant, Warne Nunn, agreed as long as the crowds remained on the beach. Officials – with the exception of the mayor and police chief, who felt a concert would be giving in to the youths – thought the idea of putting the band on the roof of the Pypo Club was a good one.

Under the watchful eye of state troopers and with National Guardsmen positioned on the rooftops, three student leaders appealed for money over a civil defense emergency truck public address system.

Roy "Smitty" Smith, the manager of the nearby Seasider Hotel pitched in; even the police superintendent donated to the band fund. He justified his decision: "If we are hard-nosed," Maison said, "they will be hard-nosed."

The money was less than one-third of the group's usual fee, but they agreed to go along under the circumstances.

Thirty minutes later, the Wailers arrived in a truck and set up on the balcony. Musicians, instruments and amplifiers all faced the beach, while the police and firemen herded the crowd onto the sand.

Wrote the *Astorian*:

"A huge howl of approval went up from the furniture-burning and beer-drinking students on the beach. 'The best way to keep us off the beach is to come up with the loot to keep a band here for us,' quipped one youth."

The Wailers' bassist Buck Ormsby recalled the band's role in quelling the riot.

"We moved our equipment up to the roof and started playing," Ormsby said. "With the officials' help everyone began heading toward the beach and started dancing in the sand. The crowd obliged and everything was fun from that point on."

For the twisting-and-shouting kids, thoughts of rioting and window smashing were forgotten. The Wailers pounded out their signature hits "Louie Louie," "Isa-Isa-Isabella," "Road Runner," and "Gunning for Peter," an homage to the hit music from "Peter Gunn."

The band even came up with a name for their new instrumental – it became, appropriately, "Doin' the Seaside."

The music not only diverted the crowd— it tired them out.

Dancing in the sand "can have a pretty tiring effect on the body," Ormsby said. "Once they were all dancing, hundreds of people, they became more docile and seemed content."

The rioting "finally fell apart like a sandcastle on a roof of a malt shop of the Turnaround building," wrote the *Oregonian*.

Empty Broadway gradually resumed life as crowds headed to the Turnaround to watch twisting couples and singles.

"The band played, some 300 to 400 young people danced and stood around and some drank beer and finally everybody drifted away," wrote the *Oregonian*.

At 11:30 p.m. Sunday the combo quit playing and asked the crowd to go home. About midnight Sunday, described the *Journal*, some members of the crowd made one last surge at the Turnaround and Broadway.

The police said remaining youth were "discouraged" very easily in this attempt and soon dispersed.

"Some drank beer and finally everybody drifted away," they wrote.

The streets were finally cleared, wrote the *Oregonian*, and the pavement "reserved for the lonely vigil of authority."

Police patrol Broadway in September 1962.

'THE DAY AFTER' IN SEASIDE

Seaside reeled with a massive hangover from the two days and nights of Labor Day 1962 weekend violence. Something tragic had been avoided, but no guarantee that it wouldn't happen again.

By Monday morning, the road out of town was full of young, battered people walking, some limping and at least one on crutches.

Justice was "swift" in the riot hearings as defendants went before Judge Don Kempton, the *Oregonian* reported. "The file of young people in smart suits and others still in blue jeans and sweatpants continued rapidly with sentences handed out in quick succession."

Those charged paid fines for throwing rocks, interfering with the duties of a police officer and obstructing traffic, among other crimes. The only woman among the accused rioters, Betty Jane Howell, was fined $300 after pleading guilty to disorderly conduct and rioting.

Rather than pay the fine, she took a sentence of 61 days in jail. "I guess I'll take my vacation here," Howell said. "I'm a fighter. I'd do it all over again if I had the chance."

Richard Frederick Wicks, a Eugene man, was charged with "fighting" and fined $39.50. Wicks was hospitalized in Seaside as a result of the incident and transferred back home for additional medical treatment. His parents told the *Signal* they would file a lawsuit against the city alleging brutality.

'A lively weekend in a lively town'

There was a sense that as bad as the violent weekend was, it might have been worse. Coverage in the state and around the country ranged from outraged to bemused. Papers weren't sure whether to snicker or to stand back in shock.

The *Eugene Register-Guard* editorial headline read "A lively weekend in a lively town," describing Seaside as the "liveliest honky-tonk town in the Pacific Northwest."

The *Oregonian*, however, was left scratching its head at why anyone would want to riot in this land of abundance and opportunity.

> "In Tokyo, in Istanbul, in the cities of Latin America, student rioters have political motivation. But in Seaside and elsewhere in America, the mobs smash property, defy police and shatter the peace of a community, apparently out of pure cussedness. It speaks to a flaw in our society that calls for measures more profound than a riot club. The shocking performance of Seaside is closely related to the extraordinary wave of vandalism that has prompted police in Portland and elsewhere to adopt special measures of control. What is it that makes the boy next door – or perhaps your boy – commit meaningless acts of destruction for no apparent cause?"

Diversion?

Local residents bitterly complained in the riot's aftermath.

"The kids are spoiled," said Barbara Baldwin, a bartender at the Pastime. "Their parents give them everything."

Business owner Margaret McCourt of Leonard's Salt Water Taffy said she thought the kids "got away with murder."

Anastasio Haralampus, owner of the Palm Beach Cafe, blamed parents and thought they should pay the fines. Others thought the fines too low, and should have been in the $500 to $1,000 range.

Mayor Pysher blamed out-of-town youth for the disturbances. "They're no good. They're a detriment to the community and a disgrace to themselves."

"In the future college-age students will not be welcome in Seaside," he said decisively.

Not everyone was so hasty to blame "college-age students," and the youth had their defenders.

June Miscoe, a long-time Seaside resident and owner of an antique shop said the city brought "this tirade of shame on its own shoulders."

She said officials had been warned of the potential for an "ugly situation," but "nobody seemed to notice or care."

"I, like many others, are looking askance at those in control," Miscoe said. "The local police should have been patrolling the city. Why didn't they?"

Young people had a different point of view.

"We were just having a good time when the police came and roughed us up and gave us a bad time," said a University of Washington student. "We got mad and I guess things got out of hand."

Welles Breatherton, in a letter to the *Signal* published Sept. 6, suggested increasing Seasides availability of bicycle trails, bridle trails, and river cleanups for swimming, canoeing and camping.

Roy "Smitty" Smith, operator of the Seasider Hotel, said he would like to "extend the olive branch" to young people.

"My idea is to give them something to do when they come here," Smith said. "I'd like to have free music on the beach, foot races and bonfires at night."

Vern Raw, the brother of former Seaside mayor Lester Raw and owner of a nearby arcade, said he liked the idea of providing entertainment for young people "to keep them out of trouble."

"After all," Raw said, "the 18-, 19- and 20-year-olds will be family men in five years and good customers."

But diversion wouldn't be enough, wrote the *Oregonian*, and "none of these things will get at the roots of the trouble," they editorialized. "All of us may well join the parents of all the Seaside rioters to ponder wherein we have failed to give our pampered youngsters a sense of decent respect for the order of the community."

> "It may very well be that this is the bitter fruit of a general breakdown in the discipline of the home and of the schools of the permissiveness that has permeated our affluent society. The kids have more money, more freedom, and more time on their hands than they know how to handle sensibly. They are bored so they go out and smash things. ...They appear to be intoxicated only with the perverse joy of being swept up in a stream of violence."

Not everyone thought police superintendent Maison, a member of the force since 1931, made the right decision in advocating for the Wailers' concert Sunday night. Some law enforcement officers felt that he had "negotiated" with the "mob leaders" when he gave his consent, giving them the idea that they had won a victory.

As a result they were robbed of what otherwise would have been "a clear-cut victory over the mob," with their "godless lose morals, youth unchaperoned and under the influence of liquor," said a trooper.

Another state police officer told the *Signal* that "next we will be serving them tea and crumpets."

Front page of the *Oregonian*, Sept. 3, 1962.

INQUIRY INTO A RIOT

S easide's Mayor Maurice Pysher reached out to Governor Mark Hatfield to get to the causes of the city's 1962 Labor Day riots. He invited the governor to Seaside in an effort to get to the root of what happened and why.

He thanked the governor for prompt action and effective assistance "which so successfully broke up the Fort Lauderdale-type of a disturbance that attempted to take over our little city with mob violence and destruction last weekend. Your state police and National Guardsmen added the necessary power and authority to our small but brave local law enforcement body to restore law and order for which we are very grateful."

Pysher asked the governor to supervise an investigation of the "disgraceful ruckus, and assist in formulating proper and effective plans to assure our citizens that such a riot can never happen again."

Seaside Chamber of Commerce Manager Don Church added his voice to the call for an inquiry.

> "The people of our area have been shocked and appalled by these happenings, and are filled with a genuine desire to determine how a similar outbreak can be prevented in the future. Because we and the people of our area are so close to this situation, we feel that someone from outside of our area would be much more able to view our circumstances objectively. For this reason, we wish to add our plea for your assistance in appointing a board of inquiry or other group, to help us to keep Seaside what we want it to be, a safe place for families to vacation."

Hatfield and his assistant, Warne Nunn, offered to supervise an investigation of the weekend's events to formulate "proper and effective plans" to assure Seaside citizens that such a riot would never happen again.

Hatfield's offer of a public hearing, to be held Sept. 12 at Camp Rilea, "is gratefully accepted," Pysher responded. "I will be pleased to call a meeting of the city officials to meet with you here, together with other selected civic-minded citizens, in an effort to get to the root of what happened and why."

Even before the conference, the Seaside mayor was presenting his own solutions. At a special meeting of Seaside's City Council on Sept. 11, 1962 – the height of the Cuban Missile Crisis – Pysher issued his own declaration of war.

"Riot-minded college-age youth" will not be welcome in Seaside, he declared. Without permitting public comment, he read a six-page letter to a packed house at City Hall, waiting to hear what he might say after the weekend's events. If they were looking for dramatic action and inflated rhetoric, they were not disappointed.

For Pysher, the riots marked the start of a Holy War.

> "The recent riot is not all that prompts me to make these recommendations, the uncovering of some of the most unlawful, unbelievable, lawless, godless, loose moral practices among the young people who come here for the holidays, some very young and all apparent already unchaperoned, and all to some extent, under the influence of liquor."

Pysher suggested formation of an auxiliary police force of women "to deal with the women who assist the males of the species in lawlessness and destruction."

He proposed doubling the amount of bail for current offenses.

Minors in possession of alcohol would be liable to a $200 fine, to be billed by their parents if they were unable to pay. "Sue and attach if necessary," said Pysher.

Of the $200, $150 would be suspended, he proposed, if the minor would "expose to the authorities his source of supply" — i.e., rat on their friends.

For conviction of drunkenness or disorderly conduct, Pysher proposed setting the fine at $300 and the same fine to the owner of the drinking establishment who sold that last drink to the already intoxicated person before easing him out the back door and onto the street.

Offenders under Pysher's proposal could be liable to $3,000 in 60 days at labor for the city for refusing to obey a police officer.

"I don't even know that they (the new rules) are constitutional," he said. "But they will give the council a basis of discussion."

Again ignoring the state's open meetings law, the mayor "invited council members to meet in private."

The nature of the meeting wasn't disclosed, reported the *Astorian*, but was believed to deal with matters of policy regarding prevention of future riots.

Pysher's stance received plenty of support. He was featured on page one of the *Oregonian* in a dynamic pose. Letter-writers approved of Pysher's comments, and matched them with their own.

"Hoodlums cannot be tolerated," wrote one resident.

"Stick to your tough policies," said another. "Half of them should do a hitch in the army."

The Labor Day "incident" was nothing less than a communist plot, wrote one Portlander. "Due to the fact that this was of such magnitude, a full investigation should be applied in order to determine the exact cause of the event."

'Unsound practices'
Camp Rilea, an armed forces training center run by the Oregon Military Department, served as the bucolic backdrop for the Sept. 12 riot inquiry. The 2,000-acre wooded center near the mouth of the Columbia, located a little more than halfway from Seaside to Astoria, listed a roster of state and local officials for the event.
An audience estimated at 50 to 75 people attended — members of the press were not permitted.
The goal was not to assess blame, said Warne Nunn, but to work on a cooperative approach to establish preventive measures. He defended the decision to allow the Wailers' concert as an effective crowd control measure.
The inquiry would establish how to sense when a riot is brewing so it can be "nipped in the bud."
The governor delivered his findings and recommendations 10 days later.
The regular police force of Seaside was "totally inadequate" for huge crowds in the area and holiday weekends, the report stated. The police force should be augments with up to 20 auxiliaries.
Seaside would need to be provide more entertainment for young people, and tighten controls on teen drinking. The report suggested that cars be eliminated on Broadway west of Columbia Street on holiday weekends and that a beach patrol be instituted.
A curfew for minors should be strictly enforced, adequate foot patrols utilized in the city, and internal policing of public establishments by the management.
The report noted that housing accommodations permit large numbers of unsupervised young people to use their facilities and that no attempt is made to control the number of occupants or the mixing of unchaperoned boys and girls. Proprietors should be responsible for controlling behavior in their establishments and "disorderly gathering" should be reported to the police immediately, with penalties for violations by hotel and motel operators.
Hatfield said there was "evidence of unsound practices" in some areas — liquor enforcement for example.

Tavern and bar operators "must be more discriminating" in selling to minor or intoxicated individuals. Along with more enforcement from the state's liquor control commission, the governor's report suggested that patronage be limited to the seating capacity of the establishment. greater attention must be taken against minors in possession of alcoholic beverages and given to the rest of adults who supply alcoholic beverages to minors.

Drunkenness on streets or in public places should be dealt with sternly, and doormen for liquor establishments were suggested.

Hatfield would request that the state's labor commissioner change the state policy of issuing work permits for minors in bars or taverns.

The hospitality program of the city of Fort Lauderdale was cited as a possible guide for solving the problem. After years of disturbances, the Florida spring break capital developed a program of hospitality and entertainment.

When asked if the Seaside riot had taken him by surprise, Hatfield said the nation has seen outbreaks in other resort cities.

"From that standpoint, we have seen this development take place in other areas of the country, and it is always a potential to take place in your own area, because I don't think people are that much dissimilar throughout this country.

"In that sense, no, it wasn't a surprise. I am sure that it was a surprise in the sense that there were those who felt that Seaside had hosted large numbers of young people in the past, and they had not become involved with such major disorders, so this initial experience, which we hope will be the last and expect to be the last, was a surprise."

Oregon's Columbus Day storm was the biggest news story of 1962.

'THE BIG BLOW'

When it came time to name the top state stories of 1962, the *Oregonian* placed the Seaside riots at number two, behind the "big blow," described as the greatest disaster in Northwest history since the 1906 San Francisco earthquake and fire

The October storm rolled through northern California, Oregon, Washington and British Columbia, downing trees, flooding roadways and destroying property in its wake, Ellis Lucia wrote in *The Big Blow: The Story of the Pacific Northwest Columbus Day Storm*, a chronicle of the event published in 1963.

In Seaside, the tile wall at the McReady Lumber Co. on North Holladay was blown out. The roof of Bjorklund's furniture store blew away; torrents of water poured in during a deluge. Power went out throughout the region and roads blocked by fallen trees.

Compared to other locales, Seaside got off easy, with a "mere flick of her tail in passing Friday," the *Signal* wrote.

In the fall of 1962, the storm took headlines, as did the undefeated Seaside Seagulls, the vaunted football team that always outswung its weight class. Seaside was, and is, a football town where "Friday Night Lights" is no joke. This year they were on a roll, defeating opponents like the Astoria Fishermen and Knappa Loggers, winning shutouts by multiple touchdowns.

In a world 3,000 miles away, the Cuban Missile Crisis – the public standoff between the world's nuclear powers – was at its height of tension as people around the world braced for the potential of World War III.

A federal case

Seaside police and the FBI, perhaps out of paranoia or simply reading the international headlines, reached out to law enforcement agencies to determine if there was some kind of coordinated link of dissatisfied youth, paid dissidents or even communists. Could Seaside's rioters be part of an insidious Soviet plot to undermine America?

"We just experienced a demonstration in one of our fair cities that smells of something other than student unrest," warned a letter-writer to the governor. "The incident that happened at Seaside runs parallel to communist tactics. This appears to me to be what is usually called a dry run."

Jennie Vineyard of Shedd, Oregon, wrote:

"Why do we have to put up with communists until they walk in someday and take over? ... I submit that we should get out of the United Nations, but fast, and quit giving the commies every advantage."

The "conspiracy" theories advanced to the Seaside police, statehouse and even J. Edgar Hoover and the Federal Bureau of Investigation. Who were these young people in Seaside who had shown such wanton disregard for property, undermined American values, and threatened our nation's future?

Investigators drilled down with a nationwide search, reaching out to law enforcement agencies throughout the country for arrest records, files and possible links to efforts to subvert the country.

Police departments cross-referenced names of those charged in Seaside for a possible mastermind, spy or covert agent.

The results harvested showed little evidence of espionage near or far, but only "little minnows and baitfish."

Kirkland, Washington, police responded to the Seaside request with information of traffic infractions and "Drunk juvenile – released to parents."

Seventeen Seattle men had been arrested by Seaside police over the 1962 Labor Day weekend. In response to the chief's request for arrest details, Seattle police related a traffic violation and an overdrawn check.

The Multnomah County Sheriff's Department provided six names of young people mostly involved in various traffic charges.

Another had been charged with "pimping"– defined as "bringing two people together for immoral purposes."

An FBI report offered a profile of a Barstow, California man, who pleaded guilty to being drunk on a public street in Seaside, had been arrested in Barstow, Reno, and Los Angeles, mostly for loitering or drunkenness.

One disorderly conduct arrest led to a report from the bureau that the accused had been arrested twice before, once for possessing a forged instrument and as a minor, of possession of alcohol.

Another arrestee had a record of possession of stolen property in Portland and a liquor charge.

The most serious offender associated with the Seaside 1962 riot had served jail time at Oregon State Penitentiary for second-degree murder.

The reports from Washington, D.C. and big cities throughout the Northwest did little to support the fears of organized communist infiltration. Most of those arrested had no previous record.

'Get tough'

Parents of those arrested were outraged at what they saw as civil rights outrages and unbearable jail conditions.

A Tacoma man received his court appearance in his jury trial notice via Western Union while he recovered at Madigan General Hospital.

Conditions at Seaside jail were, as many of those arrested were quick to assert, abysmal.

During the riots, cells were crammed with 15 people in a space designed for two. Those arrested received only a single sandwich in 18 hours of confinement. The toilet was flushed only twice in that time period, they alleged.

A Vancouver, Washington, woman wrote the governor objecting to the "hundreds of innocent people who were hosed down like animals and thrown in jail."

Her son and a friend had come to Seaside after fishing. Within five minutes, she said, they were hosed with water. Her son threw his arm up to cover his face at the force of the water. "It's amazing they didn't have to be taken to a hospital after being in that wet so long."

Elmer Anderson, a jewelry store owner from Portland, wrote a letter to the governor protesting the treatment of his nephew, Roger Allan Fox, in Seaside.

Fox, 18, had just returned from Formosa – today known as Taiwan – where his father was with the U.S. Air Force. He was at his hotel with a friend at about 11:45 talking to the motel owner when the police "rove by, stopped and hauled them off to jail for no apparent reason – hitting them with an axe handle on the way.

Fox said he and his friend were never a part of the riot trouble.

In October, Oregon legislator, Democratic Party factotum and former American Civil Liberties Union board member, Keith Skelton, entered the picture, offering a vigorous defense for several of the young people. He ripped apart the city's case against three young people who had been eating at the Seaside Grill on Sept. 2, 1962.

With a Seaside police officer on the witness stand, city attorney Nicholas Zafiratos asked why the three boys had been arrested. The officer said one boy refused to leave. The other two did not budge, so all three were arrested.

Cross-examined by defense attorney Skelton, the officer admitted he did not recognize the boys on trial.

Asked whether, during the arrest, there was anything about the three boys to suggest that they were "dangerous people," the officer replied, "It was my opinion that any group of young people could be dangerous."

Without a positive identification or a specific criminal act, the judge dismissed charges against all three defendants.

The failure to make court cases stick, the complex range of causes and divisiveness among Seaside businesses and residents delayed immediate action, including Pysher's proposals to enact stiffer fines, jail sentences and legal consequences.

The mayor's recommendations immediately ran into objections on the grounds that if adequately enforced city ordinances already would accomplish his objectives. Other of the mayor's recommendations violated the city charter or ran contrary to state laws.

Of 137 arrests made in the Labor Day weekend, city judge Don Kempton said that 98 forfeited bail, about a fourth pleaded guilty and fined. About 10 appealed to a higher court, but most of them failed to complete the appeal and forfeited bail.

Many of the arrested pleaded guilty or forfeited bail, but some asked for trials. "The first few to come to trial were convicted and fined, but when the American Civil Liberties Union of Oregon announced it would defend some of the rioters, the convictions suddenly stopped."

Kempton evidently disappointed those hoping for more draconian penalties.

There seemed to be an expectation that Kempton explain himself, as he was asked to appear before the Seaside Chamber of Commerce, a weekly gathering of "City Fathers," local business leaders including *Seaside Signal* publisher Max Schafer and his brother Joe Schafer, president of the chamber.

Kempton told the businesspeople he did not perceive stiff sentences or fines – most unlikely to stick – as the answer to Seaside's Labor Day problems.

"You cannot blame college students for this trouble," Kempton declared, "It is not right to condemn the young people. And it is difficult to pin the blame on any one group."

It is up to the people of Seaside to work together "and to clean our own house," Kempton said, "Seaside has a wonderful future, and we should make the most of it. And let's not lose our faith in young people."

Commenting on the cases brought before him Kempton declared that he would, in many cases, rather have had the parents in court than the young people.

With little support for his views and out of favor with the mayor, he was to resign as city judge before year end.

Kempton's life was to come to a sad end. Returning to work as a lodging owner, he assumed the role of building inspector, a position he was forced to resign in late 1963 after he was charged with contributing to the delinquency of a minor. The ex-judge was found dead of a self-inflicted gunshot wound at the motel he operated.

Law enforcement drills at Camp Rilea.

How to avoid a riot

Seaside made swift changes at a local level with the goal of preventing a repeat of the 1962 Labor Day riots, which saw dozens hurt and hundreds arrested. How to avoid a repeat was the topic of city and statewide conversation in the fall and winter of 1962 and 1963.

The first casualty was the police chief.

The police department had been reeling since the forced resignation of former Chief Sid Smith after the 1961 election, the victim of a personality conflict between him and newly elected Mayor Maurice Pysher.

John Yarmonchik, a night sergeant with 11 years of police experience, replaced him as chief and served through the biggest test city law enforcement had ever faced, the 1962 Labor Day riots.

Yarmonchik resigned in January 1963.

The *Signal* was blunt in its assessment:

> "John Yarmonchik is a victim of circumstances over which he had no control. He was confronted with a situation which neither he nor anyone else anticipated, and under such conditions he did as well as could be expected. He was severely handicapped in many ways in the operation of his department. Within the limitations of his very meager experience in police work he is a capable officer. He was unfortunate in that he was not permitted to gain more experience before being confronted with a situation for which neither he nor anyone else was prepared. He is the first to admit that the police department at this time requires the leadership of a man with far more experience in police work and administration than he possesses."

City fathers recognized the need for a police chief with solid leadership experience. They found their man in Ken Healea, described as a "strict although fair and capable peace officer."

He was a founding officer in the Oregon State Police in 1931 – he arrived at Seaside City Hall for his January interview 32 years later, "in spite of almost impassable highways" on the snow-covered Sunset Highway west.

"Healea is an excellent choice and one which should be approved by everyone in Seaside," wrote the *Signal* in an editorial.

They retraced Healea's biography, from his start on the Astoria police force to his position as a top officer for the state police.

> "We are confident that he will give Seaside the sort of police administration we need. We anticipate that he will enforce the law fairly regardless of who is involved. We are also confident that he will demand a high degree of efficiency on the part of members of the force and that any individual not complying with that demand will soon be looking for another job."

Healea came handpicked courtesy of Governor Hatfield and state police superintendent Maison, acknowledged by Pysher in a January 1963 letter to the governor.

"I wish to express our thanks to you and Mr. H.G. Maison for your assistance in helping us acquire such a qualified and experienced law enforcement officer as Mr. H. K. Healea."

Hatfield approached the military department, state civil defense agency, Oregon Liquor Control Commission, Department of Labor and the state's recreation department – the last of which suggested beach dances and campfires as an antidote to youth unrest. ("Wood should be available," wrote recreation director David Talbot. "This should be logs and driftwood brought from other areas rather than fireplace-type wood.")

The governor promised to be directly involved should future incidents occur. During a riot situation, he would "issue specific commands and inform everyone of what is going on."

Along with the appointment of the veteran state police officer, Hatfield offered assistance to the city to avoid future riots, with the governor's office to take "every possible step to avoid a recurrence in the future."

Major General Paul Kliever, the adjutant general with the Oregon Military Department, proposed establishing a chain of command where emergencies would call for use of city, county, and state law enforcement agencies and National Guard troops. In lieu of rifles and bayonets, Kliever recommended distribution of 75 hickory-wood riot clubs to be requisitioned at Camp Rilea.

"Tear gas could be strategically located throughout the state and will be ready for use whenever needed," he added.

In an emergency operations plan, Hatfield said his office should issue his orders to "those who have the means and control needed to carry them out, and he should be sure his subordinates have no doubt as his authority to command."

Local officials would need to understand, the governor wrote, that command activity at the local level "shall be in the hands of the governor or the individual he designates."

In Seaside, the moves inspired optimism.

"It now seems certain that many beneficial changes are going to be made in connection with the municipal government, especially our ordinances, penalties and their enforcements" Pysher said in his 1963 annual report to residents. "We are now assured of the blessing and support of the governor's office and the state police department, together with the county officials, to where I feel it would only be foolishness for any group of outsiders to attempt another riotous operation against Seaside."

'Frightening penalties'
On Jan. 31, 1963, City Attorney Nick Zafiratos, at the request of the police committee, proposed new ordinances designed to give the police department "better control of disorder on the part of over-exuberant visitors."
Zafiratos even made a field trip to Palm Springs, California, another vacation community which regularly faced large, rambunctious crowds of students.
The attorney cited three ordinances that might be applied to Seaside: holding parents responsible for their children's behavior, requiring uniformed policemen at the doors of dance halls, and requiring bartenders to register with the police department before they start work. Violations included jail time and fines.
Seaside took the Palm Springs guidance and added measures of its own. Taking a page from the Palm Springs playbook, the mayor advocated uniformed officers at the doors of all bars and dance halls.
Pysher argued that the mere threat of a fine of $1,000 plus the jail sentence would deter anyone from providing minors with liquor.
His agenda included a string of new laws.
Changes to hotel and motel rules limited rooms to "permitted occupants," forbidding alcohol in the rooms for anyone under 21 and requiring "unpermitted" minors to leave the room by midnight. He asked for regulations to prevent overcrowding by young people, especially unchaperoned teens.
Lodging operators would be liable to a fine of $500 or a jail sentence up to six months.
Pysher's "riotous assembly" ordinance, designed to stop clusters of young people gathering, stated that when any three or more people were "unlawfully assembled" the mayor or police officer could command them to disperse.
New ordinances prohibited sleeping in vehicles, trailers, on the beach or "in any public place."

To add sting, penalties for all misdemeanors listed in city ordinances to a maximum jail sentence of 180 days or a $500 or both.

An ordinance requiring chaperones for people 18 and under at hotels and motels in Seaside would become an amendment to the ordinances passed in March.

Where is everyone?
In mid-March 1963, new Seaside Police Chief Healea was about to get his first test as the city began preparation for spring vacation. While expecting no trouble, Healea said, the police did not discount the possibility of trouble.

"All law enforcement agencies in the area, including the state police and the office of Sheriff Carl Bondietti, will be on the alert."

Bookings at motels, hotels and cottages were slow, owners reported, as "a lot of parents have had second thoughts about allowing their children to spend the weekend, or the week, in Seaside."

The initial fears weren't realized that spring break. The expected mass migration of high school and college students failed to materialize.

One motel, in past years filled with young people, was empty. Others reported no-shows or cancellations.

Seaside Chamber of Commerce manager Don Church attributed it to staggered vacations, as Oregon and Washington schools timed their breaks on different weeks. Threatening weather also cut down on traffic.

"While the first weekend of spring vacation never brings as many youngsters as the second, it is apparent that the great amount of bad publicity received, the idea that the town is 'out to get them' and in a few cases a not too friendly greeting here have had their effects," wrote the *Signal*.

If there was "nothing to do" for youth in Seaside before the fall riots, there was less in the spring of 1963, they wrote. The swimming pool, dance hall and skating rink were all closed, and the Pypo Club – the under-21 club that served as a teen center – had yet to open for the season.

The Northwest rock group the Kingsmen, fresh from their No. 1 recording of "Louie Louie," played five spring break concerts to a large, orderly crowd – nine miles to the south of Seaside, in Cannon Beach.

SFC HAROLD CLARK, Co. E, 162nd Engineer Battalion, turns back all autos at the 1st Avenue bridge. PFC Ken Seppa, Astoria, also on duty with the 162nd "held" a No. Downing St. intersection, as guardsmen sealed off Hollaay, the main target of the rioters last weekend.

Cars with young people were stopped and often turned away attempting to enter Seaside.

Fort Seaside

The year 1963 started, ironically, with a meeting at the Seasider Hotel in mid-January. with the theme, "Challenges to Youth in the Space Age."
No one wanted a repeat of the city's 1962 Labor Day weekend, when crowds overwhelmed firefighters and police personnel.
"There was a lot of discussion about the participation of the fire department," Seaside's Doug Barker recalled in 2023. "And it was pretty much agreed if there's another riot, the fire department's going to stay home. They were firefighters, not law enforcement."
In a 2023 interview, Seaside's Dallas Cook said the 1962 Labor Day riot had shown how ill-prepared the community was to handle "anything like that, with a volunteer

fire department up there in the middle of a riot with no escort. I mean, holy crap, I'm surprised nobody was killed."

"Riot scars remain as Seaside welcomes new influx of youth," the *Oregonian* wrote in March. "Law enforcement – tough, unswerving – is the tool Seaside has decided to use to end disorders that have plagued it for years."

Any outside group would be foolish to attempt a riot, Mayor Pysher told the *Oregonian's* Gordon McNab.

There would be no more entertainment of the sort provided in 1962 when the Wailers calmed the crowd on the beach with repeated choruses of "Louie Louie," wrote the *Oregonian*.

"As far as entertainment goes," said a waitress in assessing community reaction, "that was considered a bribe. The council has decided against that."

The city raised $100 to replace the ill-fated lifeguard tower that had been dismantled in the 1962 riots.

The "pitch" from now on, *Seaside Signal* editor Max Schafer said, "is for older, more stable people with families. To the extent of emphasizing families, the town is changing direction."

Chamber of Commerce President Bud Ter Har spoke for businesses in the community. "The whole town was against the rioters when they gave in to the Seaside rioters and allowed dancing on the beach."

If they come, he said of teenage visitors, "we want them to respect the law. ... We want people to relax in a safe place, not a hangout."

Seaside's concerns spilled over to the state's largest city. In Portland, 48 sheriff's deputies volunteered to form an emergency squad to meet the region's problems. The program started with the appointment of Sheriff Donald Clark in January 1963, designed to "scare off anybody."

Duties would include crowd and disaster control, wrote staff writer Larry Hildebrand in the *Oregonian*. "Sheriff's deputies have talked about such a program for a number of years, but Clark himself received impetus during his election campaign last fall when the Seaside riot broke."

Judge dismissed; youth sues city

Internal politics continued to roil City Hall, even as Seaside girded for a potential repeat of the violence and unrest of September 1962.

The police department had been demoralized by the lack of convictions stemming from the riots, Mayor Maurice Pysher told the *Oregonian*. The police said they would risk their lives to make arrests, only to have the accused turned loose with a slap on the wrist.

Pysher placed at least part of the blame on Frank Walters, who had replaced Don Kempton as city judge. Walters, an experienced lawyer, had been a practicing attorney in Seattle before his retirement. He had appeared before the U.S. Supreme Court in the postwar Japanese relocation cases and took part in war crime trials after World War II. He was a World War I veteran and member of the American Legion. Walters' tenure as judge was short-lived.

As had happened with Don Kempton, his failure to bring stiff punishments and jail time for miscreants was no more satisfactory to Pysher and his council as those offered by his predecessor.

Pysher, in seeking to oust Walters, cited the case of a man charged with buying liquor for a group of teenage girls. Walters fined the man only $10 and court costs, a total of $14.50, the mayor complained. Way too lenient.

"That man could go back to Portland and tell everyone you can 'get away with anything' in Seaside," Pysher said. "It seemed to us that Mr. Walters was not consistent and was unreasonable in dealing out penalties, not only unreasonably low for major offenses, but out of reason for minor charges, which in our judgment would defeat the intent of our ordinances."

Walters shot back: "The only evidence against the defendant was hearsay evidence reported by the officer. The officer had no first-hand knowledge and he did not bring the girls into court."

No lawyer who has self-respect would sit on the bench and let any public official dictate "inferentially or directly, what he will assess as a penalty," Walters said. "That goes back to one of the bulwarks of democracy, the freedom of the judiciary."

Walters' firing was decried by the Oregon State Bar Association. The association announced it would seek legislation to "guarantee the independence of municipal judges."

The bar's board of governors expressed their objection in a statement issued by its president, Eugene Marsh.

Walters' "resignation" as municipal judge had been requested and obtained by the City Council because he was not imposing stiff enough penalties to satisfy the mayor and council.

The statement said the action "constituted grossly improper interference with the judge's duty to hear each case on its merits, and such conduct destroys the independence of the judiciary in the exercise of unwarranted political pressure."

At a time of mass arrests in the small town, the job of city judge was especially important.

Walters' replacement, John Black, 71, was a retired state unemployment compensation department employee. He was not a lawyer.

Most cases involving those charged with rioting or disorderly conduct vanished due to lack of evidence.

The city found itself on the receiving end as well.

Richard F. Wicks, 20, and his family delivered a lawsuit seeking $75,000 from the city and police department. It alleged he was arrested without cause, "hit and injured with a nightstick, jailed without medical assistance, and never brought to trial on any charges."

He said he was beaten and held in violation of his civil rights.

In addition to the city, two police officers were named in the case.

Wicks and the negative experiences of others rattled youth throughout the state. It was cruel and unfair, young people protested.

The problem created at Seaside will not be solved by a "holding them till they rot" technique, Bill Tupker, a 19-year-old Willamette University student, wrote in a letter to the *Oregonian* in March.

"It is a social problem created by us and it will continue as such until the people begin to realize it and do something constructive about it," wrote Tupker. "Now all anyone does is make the situation worse by enforcing more and stricter laws upon the teenagers. ... The main place for attaining this help is through the family, not law enforcement. The young people must grow up, granted, but must they grow up before they are young?"

Student unrest

In the spring of 1963, the nation's baby boomers were coming of age, facing a world divided by the Cold War, the burgeoning civil rights movement, and a growing United States military presence in Southeast Asia.

This political and social cauldron stirred young people throughout the nation. Seaside's riots tracked along other trends generated by rapidly changing social forces.

The Ivy League's Princeton, Yale and Brown universities all saw disturbances in the spring of 1963, as did Brandeis University in Waltham, Massachusetts.

At Princeton University in New Jersey, recalled a student in the 2008 Princeton Alumni Weekly, more than 1,500 students rampaged between the train station and the Choir College for three hours after house parties on May 6, 1963. Eleven students were found guilty and fined in municipal court, 47 were disciplined by the college, and 11 were suspended for a year.

In New Haven, Connecticut, 17 Yale students were arrested before police drove milling youths back to their rooms. One policeman was hit by a beer bottle and one student required hospital treatment.

Some of the "mayhem" was a clash of testosterone and women's rights.

Restless teens brought mayhem to Brown, the seventh-oldest university in the United States, founded in 1764. Providence, Rhode Island, police used trained dogs to quell the disturbance on a warm night in May after 1,000 people rioted, breaking windows, vandalizing property and invading women's dormitories following an an inter-fraternity baseball game.

A group of 2,500 students at Brandeis University, in Waltham, Massachusetts, engaged in a "a brief march toward girls' dormitories," but were quickly dissuaded when police cruisers appeared on the scene, according to the AP.

Summer lull

In Seaside, Mayor Maurice Pysher, Chamber of Commerce executives and the new police chief, Ken Healea, handpicked by Governor Hatfield and Police Superintendent Maison, prepared to meet the 1963 youth movement. The season's start was promising. Over Memorial Day weekend visitors from Washington and the Willamette Valley swarmed to the coast to enjoy unseasonably pleasant temperatures in the 80s.

"The streets of Seaside were as crowded as on a summer holiday weekend," the weekly *Seaside Signal* enthused. Police reported "a very orderly and well-mannered" Memorial Day crowd.

One local merchant reported it was his best weekend in two years — "with nary a hamburger or hot dog bun available on the North Coast."

The peaceful lull would prove deceptive, and for those young people detained, stopped or searched, the tension only simmered.

The Independence Day weekend was "relatively quiet," the *Signal* reported, possibly because the Fourth took place on a Thursday; rain showers continued through the weekend.

Trouble arose Saturday when several car loads of young men from Longview and Kelso, Washington, arrived in town with the avowed purpose of starting some trouble. The group picked random fights; one grabbed $35 from a woman's purse. Police searched any car driven by anyone under 30, making about 25 arrests for minors in possession of alcohol. Another 130 to 150 arrests were made for traffic and liquor violations.

Seaside police arrested 10 people on July 4, one on July 5, seven on July 6, and six on July 7.

"A great many of those arrested were Washington youths," said Chief Healea.

Doug Barker, working as a service station attendant on South Roosevelt Drive recalled a steady business in license plate lights and taillights.

"Cops were stopping the cars on the highway," Barker said. "If you said you were going to Seaside, you got a ticket. 'You got a burned-out tail light? OK, well, here's a ticket.' Any harassment they could do."

Dallas Cook said police stopped everyone entering Seaside. "And if you had three or four guys in the car, they would go through your entire car or say, 'Get the hell out of here.' It was a different time, a different culture."

Seaside's Tod Tolan remembers being rousted in front of Dairy Queen.

"I was 14, as was my cousin Bill, and my younger brother was 12," he said in 2023. "We decided to walk to the Dairy Queen for a cone. Approaching the Queen we were confronted by six riot military thugs who demanded that we disperse! I pointed out that there were six of them and only three of us. 'You should disperse!' they insisted.

"Crazy, but we did as instructed, each of us taking our own path to and reuniting in the parking lot of the Dairy Queen. To this day I wonder at the irony of these clog-booted riot police instructing us three children to 'disperse!'"

'Rebel Without a Cause'

The pattern of the second riot, wrote Ken Polk in his study of the riots, suggested that at least some rioters may have been seeking revenge against Seaside for the treatment they had received over the past several years.

One of the fundamental aspects which resulted in the persistence of a riot pattern totally committed to the punitive, authoritarian action of the city, Polk wrote.

The accession to power of Mayor Pysher, who represented a bloc of people opposed to many of the interests of those active in the tourist industry, led to policies that created resentment among youth. These focused on curfews, road controls, beach patrols, "hold-and-arrest" policies, patrol wagons, jail, and the use of undercover personnel to gather intelligence.

The conflicts between young people and law enforcement escalated the potential for a repeat incident, Mark Hansen recalled. "I remember friends of mine from Portland were saying they were going to come down and riot again," he said.

"It was kind of a riot with no purpose, like 'Rebel Without a Cause.'"

For some, it was sport, Barker said. He recalled one U.S. marshal telling him years later, "The most fun I've ever had was in Seaside busting heads."

For Larry Kriegshauser, a National Guardsman training at Camp Rilea in the summer of 1963, training was "intensive," spending hours using the night sticks.

Kriegshauser said riot training for Guardsmen began well before Labor Day, with some of it done at the National Guard training at Camp Rilea, but much of it done in individual units throughout the state.

"I joined the guard because I flunked my draft physical," Kriegshauser said. "A doctor helped get me in. I was a staff sergeant with the National Guard, so I marched that year.

"We were trained with night sticks with a leather thong," he continued. "You could lock somebody up with it and drag them along. We'd been training for it because there was strong feeling that they were coming back and it was going to be a mess."

"They were there to bust heads," Barker said. "That's what they were coming to do."

"Fort Seaside" was manned for rioters, wrote the Bend Bulletin in August 1963, shortly before the Labor Day holiday.

A midnight curfew would be in place throughout the weekend.

Anyone traveling to Seaside had best bring beach balls and soda pop for the holiday, the Bulletin wrote. "Though threats of 'We'll be back' have not been backed up on Memorial Day or Fourth of July holidays, there is still the last big weekend for a fling before school starts. Many curious youngsters may go to the town just to see if anything happens. Let's hope that nobody swings that first punch."

The band Paul Revere and the Raiders took a leap to national acclaim in 1963.

SHOWDOWN IN SEASIDE

The week before Labor Day 1963, the film "Beach Party" played at the Times Theatre on Broadway in Seaside. "Operation Bikini" played at the Sunset Drive-In.

The Oregon State Fair opened in Salem on Friday, August 30, offering "more to do, more to view," and featuring "the Singing Brakeman," country star Jimmie Rodgers in person "with an all-star cast for the revue," performed twice daily. Governor Hatfield was there to attend opening ceremonies.

Six wrestlers filled Seaside's Broadway gym for a "Battle Royal," featuring Tough Tony Borne, Luther Lindsey, "Wild Bill Savage," Andre Drapp, Abe Jacobs and Soldat Gorky – with six men inside the ring at one time.

The rock band Paul Revere and the Raiders were a Northwest sensation in 1963, and scheduled to perform at the Pypo Club over the Labor Day weekend.

With a base in Portland, fellow rocker James Manolides, a Pypo Club regular and lead man of James Henry and the Olympics, recalled that things had begun to click for the Raiders, with gigs along the Oregon Coast, in Seaside, Cannon Beach and Newport.

While they had yet to become national hitmakers with "Hungry," "Kicks," "Good Thing" and "Just Like Me," the Raiders had Billboard chart hits and their version of "Louie Louie," recorded the next year.

Paul Revere (birth name: Paul Revere Dick, of Harvard, Nebraska) rejoined the band in 1963 after a stint in the military, teaming up with lead singer Mark Lindsay. In May, they signed with Columbia Records, with a line-up including Revere, Lindsay, Phil Volk, Drake Levin and "Smitty" Smith.

"It was really kind of the culmination of where the Raiders hit the so-called 'big time' in the Northwest," Lindsay said in a later interview.

Cautious optimism

At Camp Rilea, north of Seaside, amphibious national defense assault training exercises unfolded on the beaches. The practice brought 1,000 troops from Puget Sound to the Columbia River for the training program.

The prospect of an "unusually large crowd" in Seaside for the Labor Day weekend loomed with a five-day forecast indicating higher than normal temperatures and little or no precipitation.

"The fact that weather has prevented many weekend trips for the average family this summer will serve as an added inducement for travel during the coming weekend," the *Signal* reported.

Crowds had been orderly all summer, the weekly announced with cautious optimism. "The element which has always caused trouble here has either been absent or careful of its conduct. There has been far less police activity during the summer than in previous years. Local authorities do not anticipate anything different during the coming weekend."

Police Chief Ken Healea focused on driver courtesy. "If a car appears uncertain as to whether or not to turn," he said, "it may be because the driver is unfamiliar with the street or route he plans to take and blowing a horn impatiently will not solve the problem."

The city perhaps would have been wise to remember the words of visitors in 1962, after the first weekend of holiday riots.

"Sure, we'll be back next year," students told the *Oregon Journal* the previous September. "We won the war, didn't we?"

The lifeguard tower came down for the second time over Labor Day weekend 1963.

TOWER DOWN — AGAIN

Throughout most of Saturday, August 31, the mood in Seaside remained tense. Young people congregated on the beach as the police retained control. Only a few young people dared try to penetrate the cordon of officers stiffly blocking Broadway. The mood was "recklessness" rather than belligerency, wrote the *Signal*. "There were few indications of drunkenness and drinking, unlike last year."

Probably not more than a handful of the youngsters had any idea of causing trouble, they wrote.

But some young people were raring to fight. While crowds built in anticipation of a Raiders' concert, agitators stirred up the crowd — either to relive the 1962 riots, redress past grievances, or an instinctive urge to unharnessed anarchy.

The police and firemen kept a semblance of order for most of the day, but the down was growing by the moment. They liked the crush of people and the sense of empowerment. More kids joined, drawn like moths to a flame.

The very presence of the crowd constituted an explosive situation, wrote the *Signal*, which could be triggered by the slightest error in judgment on the part of the police." By evening, six hundred teens filled the Pypo Club. Another 200 tried to crash inside.

Losing control

Late in the evening, kids spilled from the beach and onto Broadway.
As if to taunt police – or dare them to fight back – more than a handful advanced wielding wooden slats from broken benches as clubs. For now they were content to senselessly pound the concrete and nearby stores.
Damage included broken windows at Ter Har's clothing shop, the Flamingo Dress Shop, Gagga's Imports and the post office, all on Broadway near the Turnaround.
The control law enforcement had had all day was slipping away.
Police and firemen armed with axe handles sealed off the Prom and herded young people onto the beach. The resistance created a scrum – no fire hoses used as in 1962 – instead, batons, brute force and appeals for calm.
The police chief's voice became more plaintive. "Let's not start a riot. I am the chief of police and I'm empowered by the laws of the state of Oregon. I command you to disperse."
The crowd responded with a chorus of boos, hand-clapping and fireworks.
The chief's message, wrote the *Oregonian*, "signaled a determined march from two quarters, by the stick-armed firemen and police, and the high school and college student crowd."
The Raiders' Mark Lindsay, after witnessing the scene, described police with axe handles "knocking the brains out of any kid that didn't need to be there. It was brutal."
Mayor Pysher was absent from Seaside Saturday night. In his place, City Councilor Vern Davis served as acting mayor. Sensing the change in the mood among the young people, Davis worriedly informed the governor's aide Warne Nunn and state police superintendent Maison that the situation was worsening. At 11:30 p.m., Hatfield, reached in Salem, agreed the National Guard should be used to control the crowd if necessary.

Attack on the tower

The lifeguard tower had been the focal point of the 1962 riots.

One year later, the tower — which had been replaced by the city and approved by the City Council at a cost of $100 — was the target again. Perhaps the tower served as a metaphor for ownership of the beach, a way to buck the authorities, or just a handy weapon. Ongoing conflicts between lifeguards and visitors may also have played a part.

Davis instructed police to surrender the tower rather than risk injuries to themselves in the attempt to save it. Officers retreated.

That was license for a renewed charge from the beach. In a military-style formation of their own, the kids tipped the tower over and used it as a battering ram, moving east from the beach to the Turnaround before marching down Broadway.

Collegians wearing varsity jackets heaved-ho, lined six to eight across behind the tower as they rolled it down the asphalt.

Scattering police and whooping and shouting, wrote the *Journal*, they pushed the tower at a run for several blocks, snagging and breaking telephone and power lines along the way.

Police, aided by volunteer firemen, quickly regrouped and charged the mob with axe handles and night sticks. The crowd started to disperse, marking the beginning of the end of the riot. While stragglers remained on the beach until 2:30 a.m., this conflict ended in less than one hour.

There was little assurance that this would be the end of it.

As reported in the *Astorian*, "We'll see you ***'s tomorrow night," they told police. What that expletive deleted might have been is as obscure as the lyrics to "Louie Louie."

Students mill along Broadway during the day, Sunday as police keep a line blocking Broadway.

'Wolf Packs' on Broadway

The next day, Sunday, Sept. 1, an uneasy peace held sway as groups of young people milled through the eerily quiet city streets patrolled by guardsmen and police. After the previous night's mayhem, shops and entertainment venues, including the Pypo Club, were mostly closed.

The crowd was controlled but restive.

More than 100 National Guardsmen stood on ready alert, setting up headquarters in the Seaside Elks Lodge, one block south of Broadway.

"Gangs of motorized hoodlums" traveled in groups before scattering at the sight of officers, issuing taunts and obscenities as they drove off.

By the ocean, one could hardly smell the salt water for the odor of alcohol, the governor's assistant, Warne Nunn commented. "The situation is still tense and uncertain. We will be watching it closely as it develops through the day and there will be no hesitating calling the National Guard if necessary."

The job of the city and state to maintain order was complicated by a drumbeat drawing more kids to the beach. A party was going on!

At a time when Top 40 radio ruled the airwaves and anyone under 21 was usually tuned to a transistor, the lure was seductive, irresistible.

Stations in Portland pumped hourly reports of the action, with the promise of rock 'n' roll music and a party at the beach, with a possible guest performance by Paul Revere and the Raiders, who, after the cancellation of their concert that night at the Pypo Club, waited in safety inside the Seasider Hotel along the Prom.

By late afternoon, 300 to 500 people congregated for a singalong in front of the Turnaround – by the Seasider Hotel and the Pypo both – hoping to draw out the Raiders to jam.

Skirmishes, assaults

In Astoria a detachment of state police decamped at Camp Rilea. Others established a headquarters at Seaside's Southern Pacific depot about a quarter mile from the beach.

At 3:15 p.m. Sunday all sales of packaged beer were halted from Astoria to Tolovana Park, and at 7 p.m. sale of packaged beer was stopped in Astoria.

the *Astorian* wrote:

> "Things were quiet until Sunday about 4:30 when another mob of hoodlums formed for a march along Broadway. This mob was dispersed as soon as a cordon of Seaside police was reinforced by waiting state police officers and a contingent of National Guardsmen from Astoria's Company E, 162nd Engineers. After this gang had been broken up, officers cleared Broadway while traffic, vehicular and on foot, and established patrols on all side streets leading into Broadway. The short, sharp skirmish featured assaults on police with eggs, bottles and stones. The kids built up a partial barricade of shop signs, timbers and benches but were finally routed pushed to the Turnaround, finally off to the beach, and by 6:10 p.m. police were mopping up on the street."

Police cleared Broadway of all traffic – cars, motorcycles, bicycles, pedestrians – reported the *Astorian*. Officers established patrols on all side streets leading onto

Broadway, but undeterred, "hoodlums" congregated in small groups on the side streets just beyond the patrols of officers.

A gang blocked Lewis and Clark Road, just east of Seaside, with logs, blockading the road until 6:15 p.m.

The crowd regathered along the beach near the Turnaround as darkness came on and campfires lit up the beach. Police and guardsmen looked on as an occasional beer bottle, rock or egg was thrown and the taunts increased. The crowd broke into a chant: "We want beer!"

Law enforcement remained in control in the early evening, as many in the crowd still waited with anticipation, still holding out hope for a concert – or at least some form of entertainment – telling reporters they "were waiting to talk deals with police," wrote Allen Morrison in the *Statesman*.

There would be no deals this year.

'More violent and better organized'

Sunset beach fires burned brightly when Sunday's second charge came shortly after 8 p.m.

The steadily gathering mob of teenagers migrated from the beach again and showered the Prom with rocks, bottles, boards and flaming pieces of driftwood.

Officials told United Press International that the riots were "more violent and better organized" than those of 1962.

Newspapers dubbed the groups of young people "wolf packs."

The *Statesman* wrote: "Chanting, cursing, taunting police and throwing bottles, several thousand alcohol-fueled youths threatened to take over this coastal resort Sunday."

A thin line of state police carrying nightsticks walked out into the crowd spilling onto Broadway. The push-and-pull was reminiscent of the 1962 riot, but this time the crowd was more hostile.

A charge on the Pacific Power and Light Co. substation was an apparent attempt to throw the town into darkness. It was later estimated that "fifty large rocks" were thrown at the building.

Splitting the ranks helped quell some of the violence, but police were hampered by the vastness of the beach. Kids could slip back into the city merely by out-walking the police up or hiking a few blocks down the beach and drifting back into town.

Once in the downtown fray, boys and girls in their teens and early 20s wearing "beachcomber" attire showered profanity at police.

Girls in the crowd were described as "abusive" as boys – and as foul-mouthed, the *Oregon Statesman* reported. One young woman was a ringleader on the beach, her curses inciting others to throw debris at the police.

Anything handy could be a weapon. Some of the youth threw flaming chunks of wood. Many had explosive fireworks.

The riot again flowed onto the streets, with more shattered windows as far east as Holladay Drive.

At 8:30 p.m., state police superintendent Maison had had enough, calling to an aide (in earshot of the press): "Let's move these bastards back about 50 yards."

As the order was carried out and the uniformed troops charged, young people weaved away from Broadway, slipped onto side streets and somehow returned.

Just keeping their adversaries in their sights wasn't easy for officers.

In the darkness, Clatsop County Sheriff Carl Bondietti mounted a searchlight on the roof of the Seasider Hotel, spotlighting rock- and bottle-throwers until other officers could catch them. It could have been a movie premiere, and maybe some of the young people felt they were in one.

"This town of resorts and carnival has turned into an armed camp," wrote the *Oregonian*, with state policemen, city police, volunteers and National Guardsmen in one camp; fresh-faced college and high school students faced off in the other.

Fighting back

Police and fire department volunteers were shocked at finding themselves objects of derision, baiting and violent attack.

For some, it was too tempting to resist fighting back. In the chaos, there was a fine line between enforcement and aggression.

If young people were guilty of losing control, for a few of those in uniform, this was an excuse to mix it up. It even resembled a combination of "Friday Night Lights" and wrestling's ringside fights.

The police action fell on anyone in their path. Squad cars moved swiftly through city streets, wrote Gordon McNab of the Associated Press, halting pedestrians and motorists.

Oregon Journal reporter Marge Davenport told of being clubbed after she identified herself. Davenport described "almost hysterical, club-wielding, gun-toting Seaside police."

> "Anyone who got in their way was liable to get 'rapped,' regardless of his business and whether he was participating in the riot or just trying to get out of the way. The language of many of those was abusive, whether they were addressing teenagers or vacationing citizens who happened to be spending the weekend at the resort city."

In a 2023 interview, former guardsman Larry Kriegshauser remembered being stationed in front of the Elks Lodge on Avenue A, one block south of Broadway. A guardsman menacingly slid his baton back and forth in his hand as rioters passed and taunted the officers and guardsman.
"This one guy keeps going by on a motorcycle, shouting all kinds of profanities," Kriegshauser said.
About the third time he came around, the guardsman put it right into the front end of the spokes, he recalled. "The guardsman turns around, looks at me and says, 'I think you better call for some help. I think the sonofabitch is hurt.'"
The National Guard was there "to bust heads," said Seaside's Doug Barker. "That's what they were there to do."
According to newspaper reports, even a U.S. marshal, Paul Kearney, was held by local police as a rioter, after local officers scoffed at his law enforcement credentials. "You'll have to do better than that," Kearney was told.

'Badly frightened'

Residents in the nearby area had no idea what was going on until it was in their own back yards. Homeowner Gay Reynolds found it necessary to phone Governor Hatfield for protection at his South Prom home after groups of young people were scattered by police Sunday night.
The homeowner found his home "virtually surrounded after the mob had been dispersed."

Fleeing rioters not only trespassed, but threw rocks at his home and hit a guest with a rock. Reynolds was unable to get immediate aid because the harassed police force was answering calls all over Seaside.

In his distress, Reynolds was actually able to reach Hatfield on the phone. Hatfield told him that he had the impression received from his representatives that "everything was under control."

It clearly wasn't, according to Reynolds, and Hatfield responded by sending a state police detachment to Reynolds's home. The crowd was dispersed again – although "the rioters were simply moved to a new location as far as Gay could see."

Other homeowners, including Harriet Van Belzer, said rioters had "invaded" her Avenue C property, three blocks south of Broadway. Windows were broken in her home and youths were "all over the place."

"Mrs. Van Belzer, who was unable to obtain any help immediately, was badly frightened," wrote the *Signal*.

People peered from behind darkened windows, suspicious of any unusual sound or movement. Who knew who might be lurking nearby?

A woman, still in her nightclothes, who lived in an apartment above a grocery store looted for beer begged guardsmen not to leave until they had searched the entire building.

At midnight, the last of three major battles appeared in the mop-up stage as the force of 50 police officers hunted down straggling students on the sand in front of the Seasider Hotel.

According to the Associated Press, a powerful spotlight atop army jeeps "cut down straggling students and ran them to the ground like hunted rabbits. Foot soldiers swinging axe handles moved into make the arrests."

Arrests climbed to 70 for charges of rioting, unlawful assembly and disturbing the peace. Action flared intermittently until 2 a.m. guards remained overnight to protect the power company substation.

With Labor Day Monday, this three-day weekend wasn't over yet.

Riots similar to those in Seaside occurred throughout the nation, including this in Hampton Beach, New Hampshire.

Monday, Sept. 2, 1963

When Seaside erupted over Labor Day weekend 1963, other cities around the nation were facing a surge in unrest.

Seaside was one of several resort communities to face "youthful mobs," including an Ocean City Maryland, scuffle involving one thousand high school and college students who tried to turn back a clock as curfew hour approached. "One ambitious youth shimmied up the pole and yanked a number of wires loose," read a newspaper report.

In Hampton Beach, New Hampshire, a "wild melee" broke out in the beach resort town Sunday night and police called in fire hoses and then tear gas to quell 10,000 young demonstrators, according to the Hampton Historical Society.

According to national wire reports, a policeman was reportedly hit on the face with an exploding firecracker, and the city's police chief said more than 100 officers, including state troopers and military police, were at the scene at midnight.

"No serious damage was reported but windows were broken and several persons were arrested. Several persons were struck by stones and several arrests were made."

The Hampton Beach police chief said the demonstrations over the Labor Day weekend were caused by renters who leased cottages then invited scores of friends. Police took to a public address system shortly before 11 p.m.

In order to keep everyone off the streets, the main thoroughfare, Ocean Boulevard, was cleared within half an hour, but the demonstrators flooded onto the beach and when ordered from there with the help of fire hoses gathered again on side streets. Hydro-racing in Coeur d'Alene, Idaho. Unrest in 1961 and 1963 spilled onto downtown streets.

In Seaside, even as many in the weekend crowd left to big cities or campuses, police contingents remained on duty and National Guardsmen on call in case of more trouble.

One Seaside officer and several young men, "presumably hoodlums hurt in the riot," also required medical care at Seaside Hospital.

Bill Andrews was an eyewitness to the ratcheted up security.

"On that weekend, there were National Guard soldiers with rifles on nearly every roof in the downtown and police on the ground. I was scared. "I have not seen any other situation like this in my life except overseas along the Berlin Wall in the 1970s."

Kids milling the Prom held out hope for a rock concert by Paul Revere and the Raiders – still holed up in the Seasider Hotel despite an impatient hotel manager eager to see them leave. ("I just can't take any more kids," the manager said. "It may not have been their fault, but they attract too many others.")

They found an unlikely ally in the mayor, back on the scene after a two-day absence during the worst of the fighting.

Pysher's advocacy of a concert on the beach was a reversal from his 1962 position, when he had opposed the Wailers impromptu performance atop the roof of the Pypo Club building, a concert that ultimately quelled the crowd.

He was alone in supporting the 1963 concert idea. This time he was opposed by the police chief and businessmen from the Seaside Chamber of Commerce, who had had enough activity for one weekend.

Healea flatly vetoed the idea and forbade any dancing even on the beach. He told band members any musician would be jailed if they played.

Teens griped that they had been promised a dance one minute and the next minute police "charged the beach and started clobbering and carting kids off to jail."

The Labor Day 1963 Seaside riots ended on the Promenade late Monday night not with a bang but with a whimper, the *Oregonian's* Peter Tugman wrote.

Police arrested more than 70 people and property damage at homes and businesses climbed to $100,000. Damage to equipment at the Pacific Power and Light Company was described as substantial.

As the teenagers left, Pysher, Chief Healea, businessmen, clergy, parents and residents drew battle lines in an attempt to fix the blame.

Rumors of a mayoral recall movement began circulating Monday afternoon, just as Healea was proposing his last-minute concert.

The "battle of the beach" was about to be replaced by "the battle of City Hall."

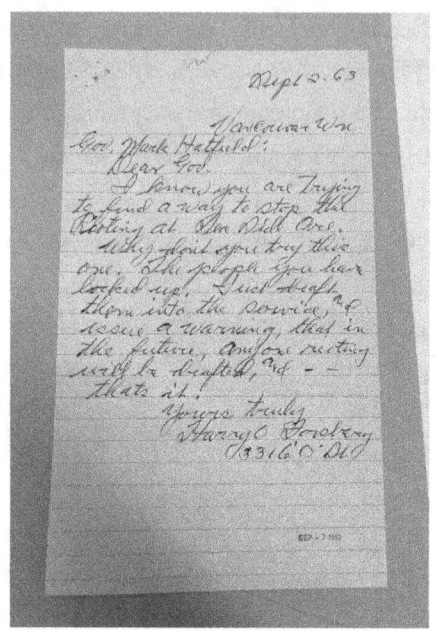

One of many letters received by Governor Mark Hatfield following the 1963 riots.

BLAME GAME

The year 1963 saw shocking news around the nation and the globe.

On Tuesday, Sept. 3, under the direction of Governor George C. Wallace, Alabama troopers turned back Black students to stall integration at Tuskegee High School.

That same day, President John F. Kennedy warned the president of South Vietnam repression of Buddhists by the government of Ngo Dinh Diem could mean loss of the U.S.-support in the war against communism.

In Seaside, the tide of youths, noise of crashing glass and screaming mobs from the uncontrolled weekend was replaced by the calming sound of breakers rolling onto the beach.

Low tides brought a surge of tourists out for the region's famed clam-digging. Businessmen cleaned up debris and sought to determine how much income they had lost during what usually is one of the city's season's most profitable weekends.

By Tuesday, 13 out of about 60 of the young people arrested remained in Clatsop County Jail in Astoria, the rest held in Seaside's city jail or released on bail.

Young men held in county jail Tuesday morning declined to identify themselves or say where they were from when questioned by an *Astorian* reporter.

Several said they had been accused of throwing rocks, but all denied they had done so.

"All claimed innocence of wrongdoing and said they were just looking on," the *Astorian* reported.

City Attorney Nicholas Zafiratos set a special session of Seaside Municipal Court to hear the first of an estimated 60 misdemeanor cases arising out of the riot. Fines ranged from $60 to $100; one 18-year-old Portland man was fined $104.50 for disorderly conduct and liquor possession. A 20-year-old Kelso, Washington, man was fined $50 after being arrested for being on a roof above the city police garage ramp. He told the judge he had gone to the roof to get his billfold. The billfold was still there when police went looking.

Bail was arranged and parents arrived to take several juveniles home.

Bars and the sale of packaged beer resumed Tuesday morning.

As Broadway returned to quiet, merchants counted their losses and surveyed damage at the U.S. National Bank, the post office, a furniture store and the electric substation.

Everyone pointed fingers and everyone was a target: the youth, the mayor, the police chief, the governor, parents and even the media – the owner of the Ocean Vista Grocery mentioned the damage done by "disc jockeys" throughout the Northwest, who "should be asked to stop building this thing up when trouble starts."

Signal publisher Max Schafer saw the days of unrest as a failure of the state to step up.

In the future, Seasiders could not depend upon anything but themselves. He quoted Warne Nunn, assistant to Governor Hatfield, as saying that "the people of Seaside are reaping the harvest of their own actions of the past 20 and 30 years."

'Violent passions'

The press recognized the complexity of the events in the face of intense emotional reactions from businesses, residents, young people and law enforcement.

The committee faced division within Seaside itself, wrote the *Astorian*, "sharpened by conflict and bitterness."

The investigating committee has "a job on its hands," the *Signal* wrote. "To say that Seaside faces a critical situation is the understatement of the year. If we are to arrive at a practical solution it must be done on the basis of competent investigation conducted in a reasonable manner and free from the violent passions aroused during the past few days."

This time, the investigation would be more thorough and far-reaching than the one following the 1962 Labor Day riots.

"It will have to take into consideration policies of the state administration," the *Signal* editorialized. "We'll have to find out just what went wrong. Why were not the lessons we felt we had learned a year ago acted upon?"

Blame came from all quarters.

A representative of the bartender's union said that the city had failed to heed recommendations from their 1962 experience.

The Reverend Father Nicholas Deis of Seaside's Catholic parish, blamed parents. "Most of these punks have not been given home training," he opined. "I have to keep my dogs on leash but they're permitted to run wild."

Big cities like Portland and Seattle were also to blame, sending "their trash" to Seaside, Deis wrote.

In a letter to the editor, a Seaside man said that it was businesspeople to blame for failing to provide "what the customer wants," whether it be a street dance, organized athletics, fireworks, a bonfire, "or what have you.

"It is up to the merchants to supply it if they wish to make money."

The *Oregon Journal's* Marge Davenport was on the ground in Seaside over the weekend. She had harsh words for overzealous law enforcement. While praising the Oregon State Police for restraint, "it seemed safer among the rioting teenagers at Seaside during the weekend than with the almost hysterical, club-wielding, gun toting Seaside city police," she wrote.

Volunteers in the fire department were "abusive" addressing teenagers or vacationing citizens who happened to be spending the weekend, Davenport wrote. A truck manned by city authorities had roared down Broadway for no reason other than to scatter children and spectators. "Anyone who got in their way was liable to get rapped regardless of his business and whether he was participating in the riot or just trying to get out of the way."

The lack of a clear response led to confusion. One youth said city officials had "promised to hold a dance and then the next minute they charged the beach and started clobbering and carting kids off to jail."

Oregon Journal photographer Herb Alden told of being clubbed by a policeman after he identified himself.

Pysher under fire

In Seaside City Hall, the mayor, the City Council, and a newly formed Citizens Committee largely representing the city's chamber of commerce and the junior chamber, squared off in apparent fix in an apparent attempt to what UPI described as "fix the blame."

Chamber president W.H. "Bud" Ter Har immediately ordered a special meeting "to investigate the fracas," the *Signal* announced.

The committee hoped to compile evidence which would provide a complete picture of the riots and their aftermath.

Mayor Maurice Pysher stood in the crosshairs in days and weeks to follow.

The day after the riots, he told United Press International that a few "professional trouble starts, communist-inspired and instructed," led the mobs and touched off the weekend riots. He criticized state laws that tie the hands of law enforcement officers where minors are involved.

Members of the Jaycees who advocated the recall claimed that they were not seeking a scapegoat for the Labor Day riots but had considered a recall vote for a long time.

The petition accused Pysher and his administration of leading the public to believe proper measures were being taken to ensure a second Labor Day riot would not reoccur.

They charged Pysher with failing to provide strong or consistent leadership of the City Council and community in general.

Pysher, they said, was unable to maintain an adequate liaison with commissioners and officers, resulting in "a complete lack of understanding of the problems surrounding the riot situation."

The letter charged Pysher with providing the press with "inconsistent, irresponsible and often inaccurate statements regarding many phases of his Seaside's government and its citizens."

Pysher refused to resign and demanded a bill of particulars giving the reasons for the request. "He consistently refused to make any comment other than he has no intention of resigning," the *Signal* wrote.

At the Sept. 10 council meeting, an overflow crowd waited through routine business to make public comment, only to have Pysher pound the gavel for adjournment before offering the audience a chance to speak.

"The meeting was opened as usual and carried on according to the routine rules of order under which it has been the habit of mayors to ask before the conclusion of a meeting for comments from the audience."

The stunned audience "quietly left the hall," the *Signal* wrote, deprived of their right to speak.

While he chose not to speak with the local newspapers the *Signal* or the *Astorian*, the 71-year-old mayor was more voluble in a telephone interview with the *Oregonian*. Pysher "was in good humor," they wrote.

The committee "needed a scapegoat," Pysher told the *Oregonian*. "As of right now, I have no reason to resign."

The names on the petition, he said, were the same people who opposed him when he took office in 1961. He said those signing the petition didn't represent the majority of voters and promised to fight any recall election.

"I have one more year to serve if they don't kick me out," Pysher said. "I might have a lot of fun going fishing. I'm kind of behind in my fishing right now."

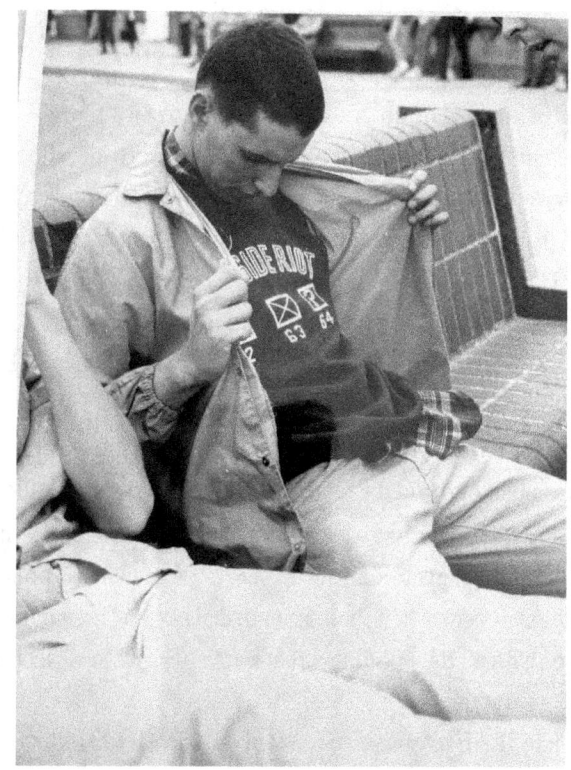

Young man displays "Seaside Riot" t-shirt.

KIDS IN SHINY CADDIES

After the violent events of Aug. 31 and Sept. 1, the response to the second year of Labor Day riots was no longer just a "Seaside matter." The recall election and divisions between mayor, council and businesses was peaking. Many saw the 1963 riots as part of a broader pattern of youth disintegration. This was the year before the Beatles arrived in America; only weeks before JFK was assassinated and the Vietnam War was about to explode. Drunken kids in madras shirts and boat shoes listening to obscene lyrics over and over again made the Establishment seethe.

The privileged attitudes of the rioters annoyed some residents.

One senior citizen, William Baxter, wrote to Governor Hatfield, that kids were "running around in a Caddy sports car."

"Where do kids get money to drive a sports car like that?" he asked. "And where did the kids get the money for liquor and to pay the fines?"

(In a postscript, he added: "The color of the Caddy is black.")

For Baxter, most galling was the wealth of the kids, the free ride, the subsidies from parents. And to drive a shiny black Caddy with gleaming red upholstery?

Letters poured in from all quarters, all with remedies for wayward youth.

A letter writer, S. Hannant, vowed to vote down the governor's education budget rather than spending it "to educate the age group involved in the riot."

Seaside resident and store owner E.S. Erickson was "shocked beyond words at the damage done to our lovely town."

On Sunday morning at 10 a.m. "young men and women, both in cars and on foot, were behaving in a most loud and disgusting manner." Why wasn't there more protection from the state police? Erickson wondered, echoing others in the community, including the mayor, Maurice Pysher. "I feel that our police department is very adequate to protect us when there is a normal holiday crowd. but they cannot cope by themselves with all the hoodlums that come here from all sections of Oregon and other states."

Marette and Paul Isle, 12th Avenue residents of Seaside, told Hatfield that during the days of the riot, their family witnessed young people in cars, yelling, swearing and throwing things. "Cars roared by, brakes screeched. Our little girl is only six years old, but this upset her too!"

Arthur Crookham, a Portland resident, blamed the state for failing to act.

"You at Salem missed your cue," Crookham wrote. "If state police set a road watch to determine whether the gang was again headed for Seaside, the fact has not been printed."

It wasn't just a Seaside problem he wrote. "They came from all over the state, and even the Northwest.

> "Here they were gathered, easy to bag, the troublemakers from many towns, the hot rodders, the hell-raisers, the smart alecs who race up and down streets and highways ....all this while the police look the other way. We shall never have respect for law and order unless law and order demand it."

Hatfield should have used his power to declare martial law, Crookham said, and put "hoodlums" in a compound and stay there while civil authorities pick out ringleaders. Hatfield replied cordially, but responded that returning violence with violence would not necessarily solve the problem. Referencing race riots throughout the nation, including George Wallace's response to federal orders to integrate Alabama's schools, the problems are "so deep-seated that I cannot guarantee a proper solution – I can only guarantee our continued concern and efforts."

President John F. Kennedy announced classifications for selective service at the end of June in 1963 and the call-up for the Vietnam War started the next year, in 1964. Harry Forsberg of Seaside wrote immediately after the 1963 riots: "Why don't you try this one? The people you have locked up, just draft them into the service and issue a warning, that in the future, anyone rioting would be drafted – and that's it!"

Why send the "rulers of the future" to fight overseas to be targets "while the hudlums (sic) of the likes that appear in all riots are left to repopulate our nation and breed more like themselves."

The United States military conscripted approximately 1.9 million service personnel into their ranks over the course of the Vietnam War, from 1964 to 1973, with almost 60,000 never to return.

Response

The same weekend as the 1963 riots, Kennedy conceded that the South Vietnam government – notably President Ngo Dinh Diem – "has gotten out of touch with the people" and lacked the popular support to win the war against the north. He pledged the U.S. would continue assistance to South Vietnam. A withdrawal would be a "great mistake."

"Draft them all," wrote Mrs. Ernest Dahlke of Bandon. "If all those men or boys were drafted into the arm (sic) forces that took any part in the Seaside riot, that would settle it once for all."

For those unqualified for the service, she wrote, "Some drunks, jail birds, robbers and hoodlums all have good jobs in mills and factories."

Mrs. Russel D. Reese of Portland suggested that those arrested be put to "good hard physical work cleaning up the damage done. Paying a fine comes too easy for many of them and is soon forgotten."

Oregon should take the lead and revoke driving privileges where liquor is involved, she wrote.

Alice M. Bahr, a physician and surgeon based in Corvallis, offered her opinion that young people "have too much leisure, and need some good hard work."

She added an environmental twist to her suggestion. "Our national forests are in terrible condition because of the Columbus Day Storm," she said, referring to what was called the "Big Blow" in the fall of 1962. She saw the riots as an opportunity.

"Can we not have work camps for these offenders, have them clean up the forests much as the C.C.C. (Civilian Conservation Corps) did in the Depression years? I really think a month of good hard work in the forests will be a much more effective deterrent from future crime than a fine which their unwise parents frequently pay."

While working in the camp, they could "also be taught some good citizenship, which their parents apparently failed to instill into them."

Thomas Roeser of Corvallis had this advice for the governor. "Why not give it to them with both barrels?" he asked.

"Build a bull pen and guard them like they do with prisoners of war. I would be loaded for them and have a big bull pen all built and ready for them and put them in it and guard them with rifles that work, and with men that can use them."

'Hard-working, honest boys'

Others letters offered a completely different viewpoint, that of youth caught up in the riots – and their parents.

The youth in Seaside were guilty only of being energetic and exuberant, wrote Norman H. Barley, of Warrenton, a Methodist minister, but over the Labor day weekend, "hardly anyone was allowed to enjoy the scenery or to window-shop. The policemen kept pushing everyone around like they were common criminals. Minister or no minister, I was pushed and cussed by Seaside police."

Many objected to language attributed to the police superintendent Maison, when clearing the riot scene: "Let's move the bastards down 50 yards."

Portland's Pat Hawkins asked the governor to explain "why a man in a high position like H.G. Maison should not be reprimanded for calling teenagers 'bastards.' If he does not have good judgment enough to know how to use proper English and to conduct himself as a gentleman and officer it would seem that you should do something about it."

Hatfield answered almost every letter sent to him. The governor proved a sincere listener, although his responses fell short. "I wish I could present a ready solution," he wrote Hawkins. "Unfortunately, I cannot. The primary responsibility for maintaining law and order in Seaside must rest with the officials. When a situation gets out of hand state authorities can assist as we do in all sorts of emergencies. Nonetheless the basic problems are so fundamental that they defy a ready solution."

TWO BROTHERS arrested Sunday at Seaside in riot of an estimated 2,000 young people, said Monday they had just gone down to see the excitement, and felt Seaside could have prevented troubles by giving youths something to do. Brothers are (left) Paul Caputo, 19, and Ronald, 22.

Paul Caputo and Ronald Caputo went to the press after their treatment by police in the 1963 riots.

'LINE IN THE SAND'

When 400 high schoolers rioted at a Portland football game in late September 1963, the *Signal* fumed about the press's a double standard.

While the event was a "puny affair," wrote publisher Max Schafer Jr., what was notable was its treatment in the Portland press, and the contrast between that and how the Seaside riot was covered — no interviews with those arrested, no news stories about "hysterical" police officers, and no one damning the authorities.

Seaside, they wrote, was suffering from a double standard.

"If the Portland football riot brings some semblance of realism to the Portland press, Seaside can only rejoice while at the same time sympathizing with our fellow victim," wrote the *Signal*.

Seaside City Hall did receive a win, of sorts in the fall of 1963, dropped as a named party in the assault of Richard Wicks.

Wicks, 20, and his family sought $75,000 from the city and its police department stemming from the riots the previous year. He claimed he was arrested without cause, hit and injured with a nightstick, jailed without medical assistance, and never brought to trial on any charges.

In October 1963, the court dropped the city as a defendant in the $75,000 lawsuit. While the city was no longer a defendant, wrote the *Oregonian*, the city would continue to stand by the other two defendants.

Caught in the action

Two Portland brothers, Ronald, 22, and Paul Caputo, 19, were perhaps emblematic of those at the scene – clean-cut youth in "beachcomber" garb, charged with riotous assembly and drunkenness.

Seaside police patrolman Ottie E. Nabors, in an officer's report delivered almost a year later, described the timeline in detail.

Nabors and reserve officer Morris Ray were assigned duty at the Turnaround. A large crowd of "approximately 200 to 250 boys and girls in the area, in groups of approximately 10 to 15 was forming and appeared to be getting unruly. Some were cheering, singing and making catcalls."

According to Nabors, Chief Ken Healea was at the scene in the city emergency truck with a loudspeaker, and had just finished his proclamation asking the crowd to disperse when Nabors and Ray arrived.

Ray and Nabors stationed themselves on the south side of Broadway at the Turnaround.

The Caputos had come to Seaside lured by the prospect of a Raiders' concert, they told Ann Sullivan of the *Oregonian*.

A friend had attended last year's riot, which ended in a dance party. They hoped this might have a similar conclusion. Paul Caputo, a June graduate of Lincoln High School in Portland working for a fence and wire works company, said he missed last year's Labor Day and had never seen a riot before.

According to newspaper reports, Ronald Caputo made his "$254.50 mistake" – the amount of his fine – when he picked up a piece of a broken swing seat and drew a long line in the sand. Then he waved the stick in a distinctly unfriendly manner and invited the police to step across the line using extremely abusive and obscene language.

He told Judge John Black he came out, like other young people, to see the fun. He drew the line in the sand "just to be drawing a line in the sand."

"We were just going down for a couple of hours and then come back," he said. "Yes, things were being thrown. But I didn't see any reason to run from them. I should have because I didn't like that spell in jail."

The riot, he said, was started by troublemakers comprising perhaps 10% of the crowd. The other Caputo brothers backed up his testimony, but Judge Black found him guilty anyway.

Recall petition

By mid-October, the "Recall Mayor Pysher" movement was underway, started the month before when the Jaycees and members of the Chamber of Commerce delivered a petition signed by 69 members seeking his resignation.

The petition repeated the charges brought by the Jaycees the previous month: failure of leadership, failure to maintain proper liaison with appointed officials, and inconsistent and inaccurate statements. Mayor Pysher had failed to provide strong and consistent leadership and went on to claim that he demonstrated a lack of understanding of problems surrounding the riot situation.

"Those bringing the petition charged that there was a breakdown of communication with state officials and others, and the public had been led erroneously to believe that adequate measures had been taken to prevent disorders and that he had continuously provided the press with inconsistent statements."

More than 270 signatures out of the 320 necessary for a 1964 ballot measure were collected by early November.

The recall effort intensified city divisions. Those in favor of recall no longer had confidence in the mayor – if they ever had. Pysher, never at a loss for words, pooh-poohed the challenge.

"Let's be honest with ourselves. Is this recall movement inspired by those deeply interested in community harmony and cooperation for the good of Seaside, or is it the result of a three-year personal hatred controlled from behind the scenes?"

In a statement released two weeks later, Pysher responded that he had been assured of adequate law enforcement from the state on Labor Day weekend. "We relied heavily on this assurance," Pysher said.

He and Police Chief Ken Healea dug in, blaming the state for failing to live up to their promise. The city never received extra state police officers, he stated, and by the time the city was faced with this "serious disappointment, we are proud that disorder and property damage was held to a minimum."

Two councilmen, William Metcalf and John Royce, signed the statement, as did city auditor Don Church.

"Not accurate" was the response from the governor, who said that 50 troopers were available, waiting immediate call for service in Seaside.

"It was explained to Mayor Pysher that Seaside would receive help when it was asked for."

Warne Nunn, offered a conciliatory note – the state would work out plans to prevent more riots next Labor Day with Seaside officials.

Image-conscious

Pysher responded to the recall movement by going on the offense, choosing a familiar target, the former mayor, Lester Raw, and his brother Vern Raw, owner of the Seasider Hotel.

Two boys from Yakima, Washington, both under the age of 18, had checked into the hotel, in violation of recently enacted city ordinances, Pysher alleged, and he wanted the city attorney to do something about it.

According to Raw, the clerk had checked the boys' identification cards and showed them both to be over 18. The city attorney kicked the matter down the road, but the mayor wasn't willing to let it go so easily.

Pysher accused Raw of "legal maneuvering" to avoid the charges. Pysher said Raw's lawyer, George Cole, had been able to "postpone, put off, and in general hush-hush this case to where there has never even been a hearing, and "it is now five months old."

Pysher added another accusation. On Aug. 31, two juveniles had been picked up by Seaside police at the Seasider. As in the other case, no complaint had been filed. Pysher demanded that a "regular, lawful hearing of the case be held in the municipal court, the same as if it were against some lesser operator accused of the same violation."

The council passed the matter to city attorney Nicholas Zafiratos, who said "he expected to place the matter on the court calendar but had no information as to when this would be done."

He was unaware of the second violation, he told the City Council, and said that prosecution of riot cases had kept him busy and delayed action in the matters.

In a November editorial, the city's chamber and business community realized that the in-fighting was doing little to move the city forward.

"Things must change if Seaside is to recapture a favorable image," they wrote.

Likely directed at Mayor Pysher and those hand-picked to his council, the *Signal* editorialized:

> "The present image of Seaside, which has become very bad during the past few years, has been created by not more than a dozen individuals, most of whom are well known to Seaside people. They have thrust upon the rest of the city a reputation which is neither desirable or justified. In so doing, they are driving away the finest – and most profitable – patronage that the city enjoyed for generations. Their motive has simply been one of greed based on a short-sighted and fallacious idea of what is good, not only for themselves, but the city as a whole.
>
> "This has to change. The people of Seaside must insist that those who have created the false image in the minds of the public either change their attitude or go someplace else to carry on their operations. The latter solution would be the best in our view but perhaps one more chance should be given them. But they must be convinced that the time has come to change."

By Nov. 21, the number of signatures on the recall swelled to 360, 40 more than the number necessary to bring the measure to a ballot – meeting the 25% of the voters required by law to hold a recall election.

Top 10

President John F. Kennedy had been in the region in early October, paying a visit to the vocational school at Tongue Point. Six weeks later he was fatally shot in Dallas while driving in a motorcade with his wife Jacqueline and Texas Governor John Connally.

His assassination temporarily silenced local political maneuvering. The world was turning.

As in 1962, the Seaside riots made the "Ten Top Oregon Stories" of the year in the Oregonian.

Amazingly, the *Seaside Signal*'s Top 10 local news stories of 1963 led with the announcement of three new councilmen, new police chief Ken Healea, the Seaside-Cannon Beach ministerial day of prayer and a visit from NBC-TV trumpeter Doc Severinsen – an Oregonian later famed as leader of the Tonight Show band – to Seaside High School. Other major year-end stories listed before it included cutting up a "huge fir tree" by the logging company Crown Zellerbach, a new city fire truck, and the naming of Miss Oregon. Whether from fear of creating further (negative) publicity or a desire to move on, the Labor Day violence rated a measly paragraph. "Seaside had a repeat of the Labor Day riot," the *Signal* wrote. "A Chamber committee was formed to investigate the action. Mayor Maurice Pysher refused a demand that he resign from his position and indicated he would fight any recall movement."

Mayor Maurice Pysher after the February 1964 election calling for his recall. With him, councilmen Elvin "Al" Goodman and John Royce.

A Bid for Harmony

The aftermath of violent unrest in Seaside in 1962 and 1963 had led to a flurry of blame, with Mayor Maurice Pysher and his hand-picked council in the crosshairs.

Despite occasional calls for unity, both those in favor of the mayor retaining his leadership role and those against were at each other's throats for the first month of the year. The recall election hung over the headlines for the next six weeks.

An earthquake was felt in Tillamook County on Jan. 5, 1964, and the reverberations would be felt all the way to Seaside. That must have been a warning sign.

But an appearance on Portland TV by three members of the Seaside Chamber of Commerce provided the first real tremors of the year.

The chamber's vice president Frank Coumont, president Bud Ter Har and manager Newt Schneider made a whistle stop to Portland to deliver a new riot report, a 12-page investigation compiled after four months of study and investigation by a special chamber committee.

They met with the *Oregonian's* Peter Tugman and other members of the big city press. They shared the 11 proposals leading with the "strong recommendation" that Seaside create a new image and "provide a new atmosphere and environment."

Kids with pocket change aren't the "kind of trade" Seaside is looking for, Coumont said. "We want families and we have the wherewithal to attract them," Coumont said. The chamber committee recommended a special commission of state, county and city personnel, plus two members of the chamber, to draw up a master plan for riot prevention and to see that the plan was carried out.

They said their job was not to "point fingers or fix blame," but they did say the report makes the point that a riot prevention plan made prior to Labor Day 1963 was not carried out.

According to the Chamber of Commerce committee report, there was a lack of communication between agencies and one factor in this was the absence of Mayor Pysher from the city during the riot's early stages. Ter Har said volunteer firefighters and police failed to meet the test; their quality was "very poor."

None knew the first in the chain of command – Pysher – was to be absent during the Labor Day weekend.

The Seaside Chamber of Commerce Riot Investigation Committee recommended that the city create a new message through 11 methods:

1. Eliminate the honky tonk atmosphere on Broadway.
2. Find a theme around which to mold Seaside.
3. Develop this theme in building in the Broadway area.
4. Eliminate undesirable business through city licensing and ordinances.
5. Better lighting on Broadway at the Turnaround and on the Prom.
6. Provide lighting on the beach.
7. Be better informed on the activities, historical, recreational and points of interest in our community.
8. Provide additional recreational facilities over our present ones such as tennis courts, beach recreational areas and volleyball courts.
9. Provide additional dressing room facilities on or near the beach area.
10. Acquire a machine to keep the beach sand clean of trash.
11. Provide suitable wood for beach fires during summer.

The meeting with the Portland press lit a fuse in Seaside. The Schafers – Max Sr. and Max Jr. – decried the big appearance as highlighting the city's dissension and recrimination piled on conflicts reaching back several years,

Seasiders, they wrote, were searching for a "formula which would bring peace and harmony to the city."

That was easier said than done.

"In view of developments this week it is extremely doubtful that much can be accomplished at the present time," the *Signal*'s editorial team bemoaned. 'From the standpoint of public relations, nothing could be worse than a public rehash of our problems."

> "We have been downgraded not only in the eyes of the traveling public, but in addition there are thousands of people in the Northwest who are looking forward to retiring and searching for a suitable retirement home.
>
> "Will they be willing to invest thousands of dollars in property in a community which broadcasts its need for a change in image and discusses its internal problems before a public totaling several million people?
>
> "The airing of our problems publicly is bad enough. But the implications which many persons will read into them are far worse. And particularly when the idiotic term 'honky tonk' is used in connection with them.
>
> "We are particularly outraged at the term 'honky tonk.' Anyone using the term in reference to this city, or any part of the city, is fouling his own nest. Granted that there are one or two places on Broadway which we could well do without, and a few bad spots elsewhere, the implications and connotations of this term are entirely unjustified and completely damaging."

The meeting in Portland backfired on the chamber committee.

The mayor, council, police and fire officials were outraged by the coverage. Not only was Pysher being thrown to the Portland wolves, they believed, so were they. The riots weren't their fault; they were hindered by lack of state reinforcements, unsupervised youth and permissive parents.

The city was split in two.

Five council members issued a statement supporting the mayor, calling the recall movement "a detriment to our civic efforts and the source of too much adverse publicity. We do not consider the charges as set forth in the recall petition as being sufficient cause for attempting to recall an elected official ... Much more can be accomplished for the welfare and common good with harmony and cooperation."

The *Signal* wrote:

"The TV broadcast by Coumont was considered to be a matter of airing Seaside's dirty linen before a million or so people in a manner which was certain to give most of the viewers, very few of whom knew or cared anything about Seaside's problems a wrong impression of the city."

The *Oregonian's* reporting, the *Signal* added, was a slur at police and fire departments and contained statements which were believed to give a wrong impression of Seaside's policies. "It was obvious to any experienced news man that many of the statements came about from remarks made in a general conversation and others were twisted by taking them out of context."

The Saturday after the Portland press conference, the *Signal* reported, members of the City Council, police department and the fire department demanded an explanation from Ter Har and Coumont about their Portland meeting. The chamber board and the investigating committee held a joint meeting at which Ter Har and Coumont submitted their resignations.

Two days later, at the first City Council meeting of the year, the mayor presented his annual report. He listed his accomplishments, including a three-lane bridge across the Necanicum River, public utilities extended eastward, a new library building on U.S. Highway 101, a new fire truck, and extension of the fire department building. He recapped his three years with a jab at his favorite targets – disrespectful youth and their adult enablers.

Recall petitioners met the magic number of 320 signatures in mid-January.

Given the option to step down, Pysher declined. "I owe it to the people who voted me in not to resign," he said.

Behind the scenes, predictably, the pro-recall and those against couldn't agree on much, with the dialogue often taking place between lawyers for each side. They disagreed on the number of polling stations. One city councilor said the whole recall process was "possibly illegal," and the city shouldn't put any money toward holding the election.

In defending his seat, Pysher mined a consistent theme: the "corruption" of the city and the "deliberate lawlessness" perpetrated by parents themselves.

"To a certain extent we adults have failed in our responsibility to youth," Pysher said.

He said that young people see adults breaking laws and getting away with it through "connections."

Mayor Pysher and the City Council passed rules in 1964 to make it unlawful for unmarried couples to rent rooms in Seaside.

"Why do kids break the law?" Pysher said. "They see adults doing it and getting away with it. They see so-called successful businessmen engaged in businesses which are unlawful, but through certain connections are able to get away with it."

> "I believe we waste our time when we condemn youth for their goings-on, and we proudly boast of how we fooled the cop, talked him out of a ticket, knowingly broke the law but have the pull to get away with it, or slipped one over on the income tax department, or took advantage of some legal loophole. I honestly believe many a youngster gets his attitude of disregard for law right in his own home, or from some adult whom he admires."

He hit back at those calling for his ouster: members of the chamber, the Jaycees, and friends of the previous administration.

"It is regrettable that for three years just passed, and now being continued into this year, certain individuals and groups insist on discord and damaging disregard for harmony and cooperation, which affects the welfare and actual life blood of our community," Pysher said. "This should be the proper time and place to pause a few moments and reflect back on the contributions that each of us have made to our municipal government, and to think a little bit about what others have said."

While reprising familiar themes, he did open a door for reconciliation, calling for greater public outreach and communication. He sought people with "constructive ideas" to participate in city affairs.

Along with reaching out to voters in the days before the vote, he polished his image with the state, including the governor's office he'd berated months before for failing to provide adequate support.

Pysher extended an olive branch to Governor Hatfield, whose politics were shaped by his Christian faith. Pysher joined the governor's committee of mayors throughout the state to establish an annual prayer breakfast; Pysher joined organizers in Salem on Jan. 25.

Pysher retains position

The recall election was held Monday, Feb. 17, 1964.

The results were of interest around the state. Reporters from radio and television stations in Portland were in and out of town during election day and four were on hand to interview Pysher when the results were in.

"Both Mayor and Mrs. Pysher have been ill for the past several days but both came to the city hall Monday night," the *Oregonian* reported.

A little more than half the city's electorate, 1,242 voters, went to the polls. Pysher retained his office by more than a 2-1 margin.

"It should determine once and for all that truth and host effort will always win out," Pysher said. "I shall hold out the olive brand and hope for community harmony and cooperation for the sake of our city's welfare."

The results provided at least a temporary end to hostilities.

"Both Mayor Pysher and Dick Walter, the chairman of the recall committee, have issued statements seeking to promote harmony and cooperation," wrote the *Signal*. "They must be congratulated for this spirit and everyone should work to the same end."

The chamber was also gracious in defeat, assuring Pysher and city officials of "complete cooperation for the improvement and betterment of the community." Pysher said he had been contacted by the chamber in regard to the letter and he assured them that such a spirit of cooperation would receive the wholehearted acceptance of the city government.

The *Signal* approved of the moment of unity.

"Harmony and a willingness on the part of every one to work together for the welfare of the city is absolutely necessary for Seaside's future. This community faces an extremely serious situation. One cannot realize how serious it is without traveling throughout the state and talking to outsiders. Citizens of Seaside are hopeful that the election will clear the air and that the election will result in a closely unified community."

But they remained focused on what was ahead in months to come.

"The strength or greatness of any city lies in the ability of its citizenry to work together to create this strength or greatness," the *Signal* wrote. "The city of Seaside has undergone some very trying times the past two years. The 'riot threat' presents extreme problems for which a complete solution will not come easily."

Even before the recall election, preparations were being made by Seaside Police, Oregon National Guard and Oregon State Police to defend the city from another Labor Day youth invasion.

Lyndon Johnson and J. Edgar Hoover approached youth unrest in an election year report.

OF NATIONAL CONCERN

A strange combination of national factors ratcheted up the stakes in Seaside's future peace and security. For both 1962 and 1963, the Seaside Police under chiefs John Yarmonchik and Ken Healea had fed the names of those arrested in Seaside to the Federal Bureau of Investigation, at the time dominated by J. Edgar Hoover.

In early 1964, violent unrest was a national issue – and all types of unrest were lumped into one big National Problem. The youth riots of Seaside, Ocean City, Maryland and Hampton Beach, New Hampshire were suddenly conflated with the race riots occurring in Black neighborhoods throughout the country.

President Lyndon Baines Johnson – thrust into the role after the assassination of President John F. Kennedy – was facing an election in November and his Republican opponent Barry Goldwater was already labeling the Democrats as soft on crime. The Republican right pointed to the riots as proof of their predictions, what a politician described as "a glimpse of America sinking into a pit of sex and violence under the patronage of Lyndon Johnson."

Johnson and his administration had to prove that they could keep the lid on crime and in the nation's cities.

The year 1963 had been filled with protests and demonstrations that set the nation on edge, culminating with the March on Washington on Aug. 28. The U.S. Department of Justice released a report chronicling dozens of demonstrations, arrests, sit-ins, pickets and marches throughout the nation. They included kids' hijinks, Black sit-ins at all-white diners and anti-segregation rallies in big cities.

In Washington, D.C., actor Marlon Brando was joined by fellow celebrities Anthony Franciosa, Paul Newman, Tony Curtis and Burt Lancaster, among others, in a plea for Civil Rights.

No matter that the "white kids" riots of the early '60s in Seaside, Fort Lauderdale, Florida, Hampton Beach, New Hampshire, and Ocean City, Maryland, had little in common with the urban concerns of America's big cities and segregated South. There was no rock 'n' roll in those riots, no dancing on the beach and no bonfires. Those were encounters often leading to sustained violence, hundreds of thousands of dollars in property damage and mass arrests.

To those seeking to maintain order, the national unrest was all of the same cloth: changing social mores, a revitalized youth movement and disregard for authority. No matter that the vast majority of Seaside's rioters had been college undergrads, working kids, thrill-seeking tourists or bored local teens. There was a creeping sense that radicals and activists of all stripes – the American Nazi Party, Ku Klux Klan, the American Communist Party, the Student Nonviolent Coordinating Committee, the Congress for Racial Equality or the NAACP.

If the riots in beach communities seemed frivolous compared to those struggling against poverty and discrimination, they nevertheless drew a similar response.

The world watches Seaside

With the world watching – certainly President Lyndon Johnson, Republican presidential candidate Barry Goldwater and FBI chief J. Edgar Hoover – Oregon Governor Mark Hatfield's Seaside security concerns for Labor Day 1964 spread across the military spectrum, with notifications sent to all major installations in the area, from the Sixth Army to the 13th Naval District.

Reports circulated that in previous years some members of the military had joined the rioters.

Hatfield broached a delicate subject to the Army commander at Fort Lewis, Major General C.E. Hutchin Jr. – the possible involvement of Fort Lewis military personnel themselves in the previous two years' riots.

Hutchin commissioned an internal investigation – finding that three men had been involved in the 1962 riot. Two of them had had charges dismissed, and the third forfeited bail.

All three of these men had since been separated from the service, Hutchin said. "Our official records do not indicate that any Fort Lewis military personnel were involved in the 1963 disturbance, although it is believed that two or three men may possibly have been implicated."

Hutchin concluded the letter to the governor: "You and your staff are to be complimented for your far-sighted preventive efforts to preclude a similar occurrence at Seaside in 1964."

Officials considered placing Seaside off-limits to all off-duty military personnel during the upcoming Labor Day weekend.

Naval Capt. J.C. Keatts was lukewarm to the idea of the Labor Day ban. The information he currently had at hand "would not justify such a recommendation by his board." But he did agree to reconsider the request, and would instruct staff to limit passes to Seaside over the Labor Day weekend.

U.S. Air Force Brigadier General Carroll W. McColpin assured the governor "that I shall take all steps possible to ensure that no military member of the Portland Air Defense Sector is in the Seaside area during the period in question."

Along with state and federal personnel, Seaside Police Chief Healea met with State Police Superintendent Maison to lay the groundwork for a meeting between Hatfield, state officials and the members of an action committee named by the Seaside City Council.

Along with his efforts, Hatfield told Seaside officials the state "can and will provide the assistance which is requested."

But, Hatfield reiterated, the state "cannot assume the first responsibility for law enforcement, which can come from only within the structure of city government."

He told Healea he had no doubts about the city's willingness to cooperate with state law enforcement efforts.

Despite his apparent confidence, Hatfield finished with a call for an end to Seaside's internecine battles.

"I do suggest, however, that now is the time for the Chamber of Commerce to fall in line in support of the duly elected city officials and to urge those officials to take the initial steps in planning for 1964 and in providing the needed leadership," Hatfield wrote.

The city's action committee met with state and county leaders on Feb. 21 at Seaside City Hall, more than six months in advance of Labor Day weekend. Clatsop County Sheriff Carl Bondietti committed 14 deputies to riot control. Healea commanded a force of 21 officers, including reserves, though he hoped to increase that number to 35.

The National Guard would have a sizable contingent of officers and enlisted men assembled for training over Labor Day weekend at Camp Rilea and available for duty. State police would be responsible for the area in which earlier incidents have occurred. State police would also continue to have responsibility for patrol of the main highways leading into Seaside.

City police had responsibility for the city's residential areas, and the county sheriff would control adjoining communities and state parks.

The guard was assigned responsibility for patrol of the Pacific Power and Light substation, downtown rooftops and beach patrol. They would also provide buses and personnel for transportation of prisoners.

Maison would have overall command responsibility and authority to reassign state, county or city forces as any emergency arose. The state liquor commission would also have additional personnel in the area, including law enforcement personnel from other parts of the state.

The city accepted the governor's offer March 2, to assist in "preventing riotous actions in Seaside which we expect to be attempted again this Labor Day weekend." Now it was time to tell potential unwanted visitors: *Stay away from Seaside.*

Damaged vehicle in Seaside after the Good Friday quake.

THE GOOD FRIDAY QUAKE

Mayor Maurice Pysher felt vindicated after surviving with his job in a special election. The results were only in a week or so before the city administration, emboldened by the vote, issued a blanket dis-invitation to teens near and far.

The Beatles invaded U.S. shores in 1964. American youth were giddy with the world's first and reigning supergroup were not without their Northwest influences. The Beatles" 'I Want to Hold Your Hand," "She Loves You" and "Please Please Me" were No. 1, 2, and 3 on the charts in March 1964 when they arrived in New York on Feb. 7.

The Northwest rock 'n' roll sounds that could be heard with roots in Seaside, Oregon, where music at the teen hangout The Pypo Club had hosted a string of hard-rocking, hard-working rockers had influenced the boys from Liverpool – George Harrison said he had been listening to the stars of the 1962 riots, the Fabulous Wailers, "Since Day One."

"Hippie Shake," recorded by Robert "Chan" Romero and his band the Bell Tones, had been recorded by the Beatles in 1963.

With its string of cultish working-class rock hits, Seaside was a little closer to Merseyside than almost anywhere else in the United States.

The phenomenon of the Beatles, with their long-hair, youthful self-confidence and devil may care, live for today attitude charmed, titillated and motivated kids to take risks in ways they never had.

They were saying no to the military, experimenting with weed, mushrooms and LSD, not just chugging beer. Sex was now spelled with a capital "X."

Seaside's police chief Healea bemoaned the bitter cultural conflicts at play "the results of which inevitably end up on his doorstep."

Before spring break, Healea wrote an open letter to high school and college students in Oregon and Washington in an attempt to head off any repetition of the events of the past two years.

The letter by the chief was sent to schools in Oregon and Washington as students prepared for spring break. In his letter the chief stressed the possible consequences facing students who violate city ordinances and state laws.

"All persons arrested by our police department for crimes other than traffic violations are fingerprinted and photographed and copies are sent to the FBI in Washington," he wrote.

The chief issued a harsh warning. When those arrested in Seaside attempt to obtain employment or officially enter a profession, this record would "inevitably come to light and it may well be the cause of failing to obtain the position sought."

The letter listed several "do nots" for visitors: fake IDs, graffiti marking, profanity, littering and "attempting to obtain lodging if a juvenile and unchaperoned."

The mayor and police chief planned to double the city's police reserve officers, with incentives that included "excellent training" and "uniforms."

To that end, they wrote, the city must build up a reserve force of "not less than 35 men. ... More men are needed and needed badly."

The force offered added incentives — "members get excellent training" and "the problem of uniforms has been solved."

A four-person committee would head the 1964 riot response, Healea would be completely responsible for operations, working with the county sheriff. Pysher was to coordinate the action of the council and other agencies. Publisher Max Schafer was assigned public relations.

They warned young people that anything more than a minor traffic violation would appear on their permanent record and be sent to the FBI.

Seaside went out of its way to see that student newspapers and the regular state press were supplied with a list of the rules, releasing the regulations just days before the start of spring.

The police chief's letter did little to improve the flow of communication between young people and city fathers.

The more the city railed against them, young people intoxicated with rock 'n' roll, hooch, sex and belligerence – not necessarily in that order – were only too happy to answer the challenge.

The riot became a symbol of cool – a local furniture store boasted its sale would be "more fun than a Seaside riot."

The *Oregonian* reported that one of their staffers – not just any staffer, but the fashion editor no less – was proudly wearing a T-shirt emblazoned with the words "Seaside Riot," a trendy fashion statement that made Seasiders so unhappy they prohibited the sale of the shirts in Seaside.

There was even the report of a Little Leaguer eating ice cream wearing his own version of the shirt – "Seaside Riot '69" – five years away when he would be old enough to join in.

The rules were draconian, University of Oregon senior social science major Marcus Wolf wrote in a letter to the school's *Daily Emerald* in protest of the city's new rules. "The city of Seaside's response to the riots is both hostile and negative," Wolf wrote. "No doubt the negative nature of the statement will bring even increased numbers of students to Seaside during the spring vacation. It is unfortunate that this has been the end result of the soul-searching which followed the two riots."

The letter also served as a pointer for the state's media outlets, who covered Seaside's conflicts from spring break to Labor Day with reporters, cameras and radio play.

The more the city moralized, the more young people found a cause. Just like the popularity of "Louie Louie," propelled to the top of the charts not only because of its throbbing rhythm but also the polymorphous lyric – teens of the day could be counted on to do exactly the opposite of what the authorities wanted.

The Good Friday quake

The spring break weekend was, mercifully for Seaside police and officials, a bust. Bad weather kept the damper on the first weekend of the break, with only a handful of "fairly normal arrests," the *Signal* reported.

But before Seaside could gear for the next youth onslaught, another seismic event rocked Seaside – literally.

On Good Friday, March 27, 1964, aftershocks from the Alaska earthquake reached down to Seaside. The magnitude 9.2 earthquake struck Alaska – the second most powerful in recorded history, behind Chile's 1960 magnitude 9.5 quake.

To one eyewitness, "it was as if the earth were swallowing everyone."

In *The Next Tsunami: Living on a Restless Coast*, Bonnie Henderson reports that the quake "triggered waves in lakes as far away as Texas, stirred water wells in South Africa, on the other side of the earth" from the epicenter 74 miles southeast of Anchorage. The earthquake and tsunami killed 139 people, five of those from Oregon.

"It took just a minute or two for the tsunami – greatly diminished by now, but still packing a punch – to travel from the mouth of the Columbia River to the town of Seaside, 17 miles on the south," Henderson writes.

No one was killed in Seaside – the only disaster-related death was a woman who died after the shock of the sound of the siren directly overhead.

In his Venice Park neighborhood at the north of the city, remembered geologist Tom Horning, the waves went up the mouth of the river, splitting in front of the old high school and flooding up the Neawanna and Necanicum channels. The floods raised the elevation of the rivers to about the elevation of the decks of the bridges.

The Fourth Avenue Bridge swept up against the First Avenue Bridge and blocked the river so it poured out over the southwest end of the bridge and into the parking lot where the Seaside Civic and Convention Center is now located. It filled up the parking lot and spread out onto Broadway.

The Finnish meeting hall, at the corner of 26th and Pine and across the street from Horning's home in Venice Park, was swept off its foundations.

"The next house up the river was burst open and filled with 7 feet of water," Horning said. "Logs got trapped underneath the highway bridge on 24th Avenue. That steered water back into the neighborhood, much like at the First Avenue Bridge. It also pulled away the pilings underneath the train trestle one block up the river from the highway bridge, making it essentially a suspension bridge."

For property owners, damage was mostly limited to cleanup: ripping out waterlogged and replacing furniture and hosing down floors.

But the tidal wave opened up an existential crisis for the city. If the tsunami had struck three or four hours earlier, Seaside wouldn't have flooded at all.

The earthquake was a wake-up call for a world increasingly informed by science that Seaside was vulnerable to an even more violent and cataclysmic Cascadia Subduction Zone event.

SFC HAROLD CLARK, Co. E, 162nd Engineer Battalion, turns back all autos at the 1st Avenue bridge. PFC Ken Seppa, Astoria, also on duty with the 162nd "held" a No. Downing St. intersection, as guardsmen sealed off Holladay, the main target of the rioters last weekend.

'POLICE POWER'

The *Signal*'s publisher doubled as the city's No. 1 booster, with issues praising the community and calling for beautification and cleanup efforts.

The tsunami gave them something to clean up.

Business for Memorial Day weekend was "very good," with brisk business at restaurants and more families in town. Parakiters, clam diggers, horseback riders, sand castle engineers and families on picnics, the *Signal* beamed. Memorial Day came and went without serious incidents.

Fifteen young people were arrested, with the majority involving minors with alcohol. Four people were arrested for drunkenness, three for open seal, two for minors in possession, four miscellaneous traffic violations, one for disorderly conduct and one charged with starting a fight on Broadway.

The cleanup campaign was working, the *Signal* announced. "The general weather will of course have a great deal of bearing on the business, but it is believed that the efforts of local persons to improve Seaside's appearance will be rewarded this summer," the *Signal* wrote in June.

The weekend of July 4 was called "the best in years."

The city was certainly buoyed by events – or the rather non-event – in Coeur d'Alene, Idaho, which had been marked by years of local riots during a river race. In years past, unruly youth had wreaked havoc during high-speed boat races – hydroplanes – on the lake.

"An attempt to start a riot was quickly quelled and except for a short period order was maintained on the streets," the *Signal* reported. "The experience there proves that the answer is nothing more nor less than police power."

In Seaside, the days of proposing rock 'n' roll concerts and beach bonfire parties were over. The Idaho city's quiet offered a lesson to Seaside, the *Signal* wrote.

"If we are to escape disorders which are costing this city a great deal of patronage we will have to confront the hoodlums with sufficient police power, plus the will to use it."

It was time for residents to rally on behalf of law enforcement. The editors added "police need support and sympathy rather than charges of 'brutality.'"

The *Oregonian* provided a forecast of fair skies for the Labor Day weekend. Seaside, they wrote, "marred by youthful rioting the last two years, is reported calm as it approaches the holiday."

Mayor Maurice Pysher told reporters "he and other community leaders have heard nothing about the possibility of trouble over the weekend."

Reservations were reported good – hotels in the center of town expected a capacity business.

Despite all the "good news" in Seaside – the end to the recall conflict, recovery from the tsunami – the city couldn't get out from under the shadow of the previous two riots. They prepared for a battle on the beach with the crystal clear message to young people to stay away from Seaside.

Ken Polk, in his later analysis of the events leading up to the 1964 riots, said that the rules may have backfired – leading to "more thorough planning" by the youth. Kids would bury "caches" of liquor in order to evade sales limits.

The city added punch to its riot ordinance clause days before Labor Day. An amendment to city law upped fines to $500 for "riot or unlawful assembly," with the possibility of 180 days in jail for offenders.

The Pypo Club, which had played a prominent role in the previous two years' riots, was in a new location a block to the north and away from the beach, out of the core area between the beach, the Prom, the Turnaround and Broadway. After complaints in 1963 that "there was no place to dance," the new club would hold 700 people. It would also be far enough away from the Prom to isolate young people from the beach. The city administration has "done all that is possible to meet the threat of disorder," the *Signal* headlined on the editorial page. "Under no circumstances can they be held accountable for anything which may happen."

At Camp Rilea, the military base in Warrenton, two detachments of National Guard troops attended a training assembly, available to assist in case of emergency, as would state police.

The Military Department staff, led by Major General Donald Anderson, Lt. Col. Harvey Latham and Sgt. First Class Lawrence W. Baker, led a group of five, including an operation coordinator, task force commander, troop commander, air officer and liaison officer.

The task force organization brought a 100-man force, with the 1st Squadron 82nd Cavalry furnishing the bulk of the troops under the "grass fire approach," creating a safe perimeter to prevent the spread of unrest from the beach area into the city.

Along with four groups of officers and enlisted men, the state attached two helicopter pilots, two helicopter mechanics and two bus drivers.

Two helicopters, six 2 1/2 ton trucks and 20 smaller trucks, one sedan was made available to handle any contingency.

They paid heed to the events of 1962 and 1963 in Seaside, when youths had manned rooftops, seized fire hoses and aimed to disable the power station.

In addition, 44 state policemen were deployed.

Missions included rooftop security on buildings along Broadway and security guards at the power station. A motorized beach patrol was added to corral fleeing young people. The wretched jail conditions were supplanted with plans to transport "prisoners" directly to the county jail in Astoria. Police in Astoria, Tillamook, Newport, Hillsboro, Forest Grove and St. Helens were ready on call to assist if the weekend got out of hand.

Operation Seaside

The prelude to the weekend came at 1 p.m., Friday, Sept. 4, when the military department staff and governor's staff met with the superintendent of state police and the Seaside attorney, Nicholas Zafiratos. Zafiratos updated officials on the new ordinances enacted by Seaside and what charges against rioters might be preferred.

Warne Nunn, on the scene as he had been the previous two years, "reassured the groups of the solid support" from Governor Mark Hatfield's office.

The operation moved forward the next morning, Saturday, Sept. 5, with a task force meeting at Camp Rilea. A forward command post was established at 12:30 in Seaside at the railroad station along Highway 101. A rear command post remained at Camp Rilea, with radio communications linking the two. A close liaison was maintained at all times with the state police at both the forward and rear command post, operational on a 24-hour basis.

At 1 p.m. Saturday, guards assumed positions on the power stations. ("These troops were fed on position," read a later military report.)

At 2 p.m., 12 enlisted men and officers and four ¼-ton vehicles with radio communications rolled into Seaside to act as a mobile reserve. They shared intel with eight men on rooftops.

Plainclothes riot police circulated to pick up information on their plan.

Young people began arriving in Seaside on Friday night from Oregon and Washington points, the *Statesman* reported, with some coming from as far as Utah. The forecast surrendered to overcast skies and cool weather.

Crowds of milling teenagers who had "restlessly prowled the streets and amusement parlors of this seashore town massed on the Turnaround, the *Oregonian* reported on Sept. 6.

Seaside Mayor Maurice Pysher viewed the disturbance from the second floor balcony of the Seasider Motel, directly on the beach at the Turnaround.

"Oh, it could get tough," he said. "Real tough. Those jackasses out there are apt to try anything."

A crowd of youth hurl a traffic sign at a photographer. Earlier, the youths tried to take the newsman's camera.

MOTLEY CREW

What made the 1964 riots different than those of the previous two years? In 1964, the state, city and county "got serious." A presidential assassination, race riots and the ramped-up Vietnam War led to a sense that in Seaside, Oregon, the war was at home. Containing it was a matter of national security.

The state, county and city aligned in ways they hadn't before.

While in years past they could let a bunch of teens in madras shirts and khakis wreak havoc on the downtown while blasting rock 'n' roll, now law enforcement units organized, prepared and coalesced, using modern policing and military tactics.

Governor Hatfield, in the past considered laissez-faire in his response, ratcheted up his team and gave his special assistant Nunn command power at the scene. Police and National Guard were well prepared and their tools far more sophisticated than in the past.

While they were mostly without firearms, troops had tear gas and axe handles at the ready.

New city laws were in effect to deter young people from gathering. Members of the state's liquor commission vigilantly monitored Seaside's bars and liquor stores. Undercover officers equipped with walkie-talkies took scores of crowd photos and later police used a new technology, the Polaroid camera, when booking an arrest. A select riot squad was distinguished by their blue uniforms, helmets and clubs.

The disorder in the next three days was what state officials had dreaded but carefully prepared for, wrote Peter Tugman in the *Oregonian*.

"It pitted more than 1,000 high school and college-age youngsters against well-drilled and massed police officers and soldiers."

'A motley crew'

The migration into Seaside for Labor Day weekend 1964 began Friday, Sept. 4, many described as "rubber neckers" waiting to see when the action would start.

"Everyone on the streets agreed that it was a very motley crew," wrote the *Signal*. "They were a young group, many high school-aged and many young girls."

The crowd, described as mostly teens from 16 to 19 years old, roamed the streets into the evening "causing little trouble other than irritating local people with their party attitude and general grubby appearance," the *Signal* wrote.

Teens drank nonalcoholic beverages and danced the swim and the Watusi Friday night at the under-21 Pypo Club, wrote *The Albany Herald-Democrat*.

The Pypo Club, which played a pivotal role as a youth gathering place and stage-drop for the 1962 and 1963 riots at its location at No. 1 Broadway, had relocated a block-and-a-half east and one block north of the Prom on Oceanway, a former electrical company.

The Seattle rock 'n' roll band James Henry and the Olympics, led by lead singer Jim Manolides, were on the marquee at for the weekend. The Jerden recording group – a company founded by Seaside High School grad Jerry Dennon – was known for "My Girl Sloopy" and "Here I Stand."

Manolides and members of the group became good friends with "we townies," Seaside's Jeff Roehm said, and often partied late night. "I can still hear Jim Manolides up front singing 'My Wife Can't Cook,' my fav Olympics tune." Pypo Club manager Steve Johnson, a high school gym teacher when he wasn't presiding over the under-21 club, told the press: "We're hoping for the best."

Situation report

Saturday brought an older crowd into Seaside, college students in their later teens and early 20s. There was a sense that young people were biding their time, waiting for the right moment to challenge police.

A military command post was established at 12:30 p.m. at the railway station.

A reserve force of 12 enlisted men and officers and four one-quarter ton vehicles with radios were brought into Seaside to act as a mobile reserve.

An additional eight enlisted men were designated as roof guards.

The rear command post remained at Camp Rilea, with communication via radio.

At 1 p.m., 16 enlisted men and noncommissioned officers manned the two power stations on a 24-hour basis.

To avoid their misuse by youth as battering rams or chain weapons, a beach guard tower and playground equipment were moved away from the Turnaround further onto the beach. Broadway was shut off for its entire length and on nearby connector streets.

Throughout the morning and early afternoon, officers kept traffic moving and broke up larger groups.

The kids spent the afternoon "roaming the streets," wrote the *Signal*. "They amused themselves by zipping up and down the last block of Broadway and skateboards and watching a pair of large dogs running around."

Minors didn't even bother to hide the beer in their cars. "They were not even trying to be discreet about it," an officer complained. "Many of them didn't even try to hide the beer when their cars were stopped."

One University of Oregon senior, a member of the Beta Theta fraternity, explained: "I know many of these guys," he told the *Oregon Statesman*. "They come down here for two reasons: to drink and to find girls. After they get their fill of beer, they look for trouble."

In the late afternoon young people congregated on the beach just north of the Turnaround listening to music. A small group of dancers gathered before drifting away.

Another group formed at a beach fire as teens passed a bottle around.

Occasionally, the bottle would be raised in the air, and a loud cheer would go up. They began chants of "Let's riot! Let's riot!"

Every time a National Guard helicopter would pass over, the kids made obscene gestures up in its direction.

Running alone

A little after 8 p.m., one young man tried to lead a charge up the beach. When he turned to looked back, he realized he was running and yelling all alone, "not a soul behind him," the *Signal* reported.

He stopped the charge, spun back and meekly returned to the larger group.

Another half-dozen young men dragged a large log toward the Turnaround. They didn't get far.

It was if the police "appeared from thin air," boys told reporters, because by the time they were at the steps of the Turnaround, there were at least a dozen state policemen waiting on the steps. The log never left the beach.

A lone youngster climbed the flagpole at the Turnaround, only to be met at the bottom by state policemen.

But crowds grew and prepared to advance up Broadway, ready to make a determined charge at police.

Startlingly, in response, the state police appeared to break ranks and ran away from the crowd down Broadway toward the intersection of Columbia Street.

Thinking they had the police on their heels, the mob charged after them.

The youth had fallen into "one of the simplest of the sucker traps, similar to a trap play in football," wrote the *Signal*.

At the intersection, a group of state police riot squad officers were waiting for them. The yipping and yelling mob reversed directions — fast."

Police blocked off entrances to the Turnaround, shoving the mob east away from the beach where the kids were boxed in.

Officers cleared the street by spreading ranks and marching two to three blocks, pushing the crowds ahead of them. All the while, the crowds responded by throwing rocks, bottles and loose sand.

As night fell, groups of young people began forming on all sides of the police, taunting police, tossing an occasional cigarette butt at them and pushing.

One undercover photographer circulated with young people who confided their plans; they didn't find out who he was until it was "too late," wrote the *Signal*.

At 9:30, the governor's aide, Warne Nunn, was hit by a rock in the leg, but was not injured.

Guardsmen grabbed people throwing rocks from buildings.

Two squads were called from Camp Rilea at 9:15 to assist police in guarding the beach in front of the Turnaround.

Officers were added on four key buildings along Broadway from the Prom east to Columbia.

Young people were herded further out on the beach and held there by a line of police which stretched from the Turnaround north for more than four blocks. Their spirits were broken.

Soon, a steady string of cars was seen heading out of town.

Seaside appeared to be calm at midnight, when rioters were still being booked into jail. Overflow prisoners were taken to the Clatsop County jail in Astoria.

Guardsmen remained on duty until Sunday morning at 1:30 a.m., when police superintendent Maison released them. Guards remained on the power stations and two squads – 24 enlisted men – remained at the fire station on standby alert.

Officials were feeling pretty good that the situation Friday and Saturday in Seaside hadn't gotten out of control. Yes, there had been arrests, some violent forays, whizzing bottles, rocks and sand – but no serious injuries and a minimum of property damage. "Countless" teenagers suffered bumps and scratches in the melees, newspapers reported, but only four required hospital treatment.

Seventy-five people were arrested Saturday on charges ranging from unlawful assembly to violation of liquor laws, many transferred by bus from the Seaside jail to more spacious facilities in Astoria, about 17 miles north.

Saturday night duty into Sunday continued until 1:30 a.m.

The chaos of the night and rules against lodging young people led to a few lost or in need of shelter, sleeping on the beach or "scrounging" on the streets. While most were men, some young women were swept into the tide.

A "pretty teenage girl" turned herself into the police station, the Oregon Statesmen reported.

"Put me in jail," she said. "I'm a vagrant. If you don't arrest me, I'll go back out and sleep on the beach.'

When police informed her that they didn't have any jail facilities for little girls unless they put her in with the boys, she replied, "No, I don't want any more boys tonight."

"The little girl didn't look it, but she was 19," wrote the Statesmen. "A reserve policeman took her to find quarters for the night."

Taking no chances

Officials didn't take any chances into Sunday and Monday: Guards remained on the power stations, and two guards, 24 enlisted men, remained at the fire station on standby alert. The remainder of the personnel returned to Camp Rilea.

Although hopeful that more serious rioting would not erupt Sunday night, Governor Hatfield noted, "You can never fully estimate the extent of mob violence. Most of those involved in the rioting are probably nice, clean-cut kids at home, but when they get into a situation like this they become no more than hoodlums. Whatever happens we are going to maintain law and order. We have the manpower and we will do what is necessary in order to quell any rioting."

For locals, a state of siege prevailed over the town.

Mayor Maurice Pysher staked out a location on the second floor balcony of the Seasider Motel, telling reporters: "Bullets are the answer. We should treat them as invaders, for that's what they are. If we don't use bullets the Labor Day weekend riots are going to be a permanent fixture. These jackasses are likely to try anything."

Children were told to stay at home, Tom Horning remembered, because of the "unsavory characters" in Seaside.

"I was 10 at the time," Horning said. "I wanted to go downtown but my mother wouldn't let me, he recalled. "We said we'd be down under the bridge or something, you know where we'd be safe. She said no one was safe in this situation, so we got confined and put into our bedrooms, not let out."

Other Seasiders reported similarly being not allowed to leave their beach house and being locked down by cautious parents.

'Crows lined on the fence'
Sunday followed a pattern similar to Saturday's, with young people milling around during the day – described as "a little more abusive and adventurous than the previous day.
Police arrested kids sleeping in cars, carrying liquor and disorderly conduct.
Despite roadblocks turning cars away at the city's entrances, the crowd grew to more than a thousand by late Sunday afternoon.
The *Signal* painted a vivid picture of a strange carnival day with a menacing twist. The unrest erupted into a series of violent incidents, games of cat-and-mouse with police, guardsmen and even the press.
Harry Robinson, a broadcaster with KIRO-TV in Seattle, was attacked by the mob on the beach. His clothes were torn and his tape recorder was wrecked.
While no girls were arrested, there was one who openly invited arrest, reported the *Signal*. She was riding on her escort's shoulders and trying to flip the hard hats off policemen's heads.
A young man who was running after a pool hall fistfight hit the pavement so hard he vomited – before being arrested.
After another chase, a young man darted away from police at the amusement park on Broadway. He darted in at the Ferris wheel but missed seeing the barricade there and hit it about thigh high. It flipped him completely over.
Wrote the *Signal*:

> "He slowly got on his feet and hippity-hopped away. A policeman was standing right behind him, and a bystander said, sarcastically, 'Oh, look at that poor kid.' This broke the policeman up. He stood there laughing and watched the kid limp away."

Around 5 p.m. a group of young people made an attempt to charge down Broadway under the pretext of playing football in the street.

As before, there were suddenly state policemen everywhere, especially in a line across the street waiting for them. They stopped and the leaders of the charge slowly drifted away.

At dusk, they grouped around a large fire directly west of the Turnaround. Several adults with young children went down to watch them work themselves up enough to start more trouble.

The crowd of spectators formed on the Prom and stretched two- or three-deep for approximately five blocks. One reporter described them as looking "like crows lined up on the fence."

After dark the crowd on the beach became louder and louder as they gathered around a beach fire.

At 8 p.m. the first charge came. The crowd picked up a burning log and started running toward the north steps of the Turnaround.

This was the turning point of the night and the start of the police counterattack.

The governor's aide, Warne Nunn, speaking through a megaphone, warned the crowd: "In the name of the state of Oregon and the city of Seaside, you are ordered to disperse. If you do not disperse you will be subject to arrest."

He made the statement three times, according to Seaside city ordinance and state law before state police moved in.

As block after block of the town's main street, Broadway, was cleared, law enforcement personnel had to contend with couples carrying or leading children and many older people crowding the sidewalks.

Police Sunday night struggled o disperse the angry mob for hours, aided by two helicopters from the 41st aviation group.

The flurry of action started about 9:30 p.m. when a large piece of driftwood was lit on the beach and six boys in a crowd of seven-hundred started carrying it toward the city center. Thirty state police armed with night sticks drove them back. The boys dropped the crackling log and grabbed rocks instead. Boys began tearing apart a wooden guard rail to get clubs before a charge at police.

Rocks and bottles flew with machine-gun fire speed. Policemen shielded their eyes and faces before charging down the steps amid a rain of rocks and sand-filled bags.

At beach entrances, troopers repulsed two more attempts by more than one-hundred youths to break through barricades. But it was a game of whack-a-mole as two thousand other youths gathered, taunting the troopers and flinging rocks and beer bottles their direction.

The troopers quickly formed a wedge and drove the teenagers off the street and back to the beaches.

Drinking establishments either closed to the kids or ran out of beer.

One young man was knocked unconscious after trying to escape officers by skateboarding down Broadway and colliding head on with a wooden post. Soon he could be seen coming through the crowd, across no-man's-land between the officers and rioters carried by his friends, looking like a warrior being carried home on a shield.

Race was never considered an issue in the Seaside riots, but one incident involved an African American, "the only one seen on the streets" noted the *Signal*.

> "One youth picked up a manhole cover in the middle of the street. Another replaced it. Then the Negro youth picked up the manhole cover, according to eyewitnesses, and threw it toward the policemen. They rushed in and took him into custody."

When he was taken toward the paddy wagon, he broke and ran. An attempt was made by one bystander to stop him but he eluded him too, and was off and running. He was finally caught by a Seaside reserve policeman a few blocks to the south on Avenue I. For the next few hours, police began a slow drive east on Broadway, forcing young people back slowly, half a block or a block at a time. When state policemen or National Guardsmen marched by, they taunted them with catcalls and by calling cadence.

Henry Schaink of the *Eugene Register-Guard* described the scene:

> "At 9:30, the first window was broken. The loud noise sent those near the window scrambling over a nearby wooden fence. The noise increased and the rioters moved faster. After the crowd had been forced about four blocks, rocks started being thrown through plate-glass store windows about every 30 seconds. What turned out to be the fine rush by police brought a barrage of rocks from rioters. Reporters and photographers, standing on the sidewalk

between police and the youths, leaped for cover. As I ran behind a post, a rock bounced from the pavement and struck my leg."

Guardsmen stationed on buildings along Broadway with walkie-talkies kept a constant check on the youths as helicopters hovered overhead.

The aquarium, a few blocks to the north, was well protected to prevent broken windows or vandalism. When one young rioter fled from police, aquarium employees grabbed him and dragged him through a mud puddle on the way to the police patrol wagon.

Back on Broadway the slow process of driving the mob out of town continued. For law enforcement, it was a grueling battle. When the rioters were driven to the vicinity of the Broadway bridge, they started breaking up the wood fence between the Pastime Tavern and Seaside Business Service. They used the slats and posts to break windows on the way east to Holladay Drive. Police in turn rushed the crowd.

A few young people tried to sneak behind the city hall but they were driven out by Seaside policemen and firemen. Others ran up the alley behind Broadway only to be flushed out by authorities.

Young people make a charge on the beach, only to be repelled by law enforcement.

WHO THREW THE TEAR GAS INTO THE PYPO CLUB?

Was it a tear gas grenade, some kind of powder, or something else? Was it one explosive or many?

The Seattle-based rock band James Henry and the Olympics were pounding out their hits late Sunday night when a military-type tear gas grenade about the size of a soup can was thrown into the under-21 Pypo Club, the *Oregonian* reported.

The *Register-Guard* described it this way:

"At 11:42 Sunday night, two tear gas bombs were thrown (not by police) through windows of the Pypo club as some 90 youths were dancing. The building was evacuated in about 30 seconds, according to a co-owner."

The *Astorian* wrote that it was not a canister or soup can, but a "sack of powder which acted like tear gas."

The *Seaside Signal* also described the incendiary as a bag of powder.

Hundreds of young people rushed for the exits of the Pypo Club, and many given oxygen by the Seaside Fire Department rescue unit. Only two girls in the group required medical attention. The others just shed tears and many refused to leave as the five-piece combo, after a brief interruption, played on.

Who threw the gas, and was it even gas?

Earlier in the evening, wrote one report, the National Guard had deployed tear gas to disperse the crowd. If it was a young person, a perpetrator or perpetrators were never identified.

Among the hundreds of arrests that weekend, most for fighting, drinking, disorderly conduct and lesser charges such as using profane language, sleeping in a car and urinating in the street, no one appears to have been charged with releasing the tear gas.

Quiet at last

Late Sunday night, the town quieted down and another exodus similar to that of Saturday night occurred.

Carload after carload of youths left town. Before midnight the town was vacant except for the police and guardsmen. Store owners patched broken windows with plywood. Otherwise the town looked as though it were about 5 a.m.

Rumors that young people had regathered in Cannon Beach for an "invasion" of Seaside never materialized.

Unrest continued "here and there," wrote the governor's aide Warne Nunn in his after-action report, until 1:30 a.m., "when streets became practically deserted and National Guard personnel, with the exception of the power station guards and two squads on standby alert."

By midnight, Broadway was nearly deserted, quiet again. All that was heard was the din of juke box music coming from locked bars, mingling with the wail of distant sirens.

Monday brought drenching rain and an end to the conflict.

"The streets were deserted all morning," reported the Associated Press. "When the rain stopped in the afternoon some youths appeared. Police advised them to leave town, and most went along quietly."

By mid-afternoon the danger of additional trouble was considered nonexistent. After the National Guard withdrew, state police followed.

Nunn estimated the cost to the state was "at least $10,000 to control the rioting." That was the National Guard cost alone, and did not include the state police

"That's a damn hefty babysitting bill," quipped Major General Donald Anderson, adjutant general of the Oregon National Guard.

Police arrested 108 people over the Labor Day weekend, including 11 under age 18. All were held on misdemeanor charges with bail from $14.50 to $1,000.

Arraignments were scheduled Tuesday in Seaside Municipal Court.

Oregon State Police Superintendent Maison said of the rioters: "There were as many of them as last year but they didn't have as much defiance for law and order."

Already Seaside Mayor Pysher said he expected to meet with local and state officials planning for the 1965 Labor Day weekend. "Someone must knock some sense into a riotous minority of a generally well-mannered younger generation."

U.S. Senator Wayne Morse, a Democrat, commented that he could not understand why young citizens who have all advantages of enlightened education can act in such a manner. "Apparently they have not learned the important lesson that the preservation of American freedom rests upon maintaining a system of law and order."

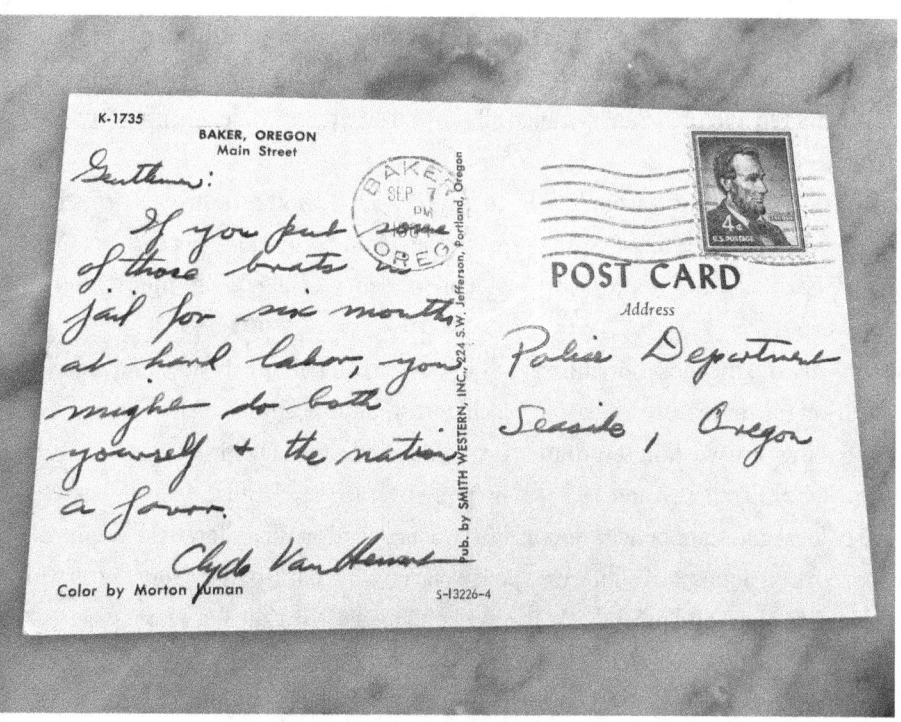

One of dozens of pieces of mail addressed to officials offering solutions to Seaside's riots.

'REMEDIES' FOR A RIOT

Send them to Vietnam.
Make them slave labor.
Arrest them all.

These were among the suggestions as to what to do about Seaside's Labor Day weekend rioters.

For three years in a row – 1962, 1963 and 1964 – young people from 15 to 25 had showed up to party and thumb their noses at authorities. Among them were college kids, high schoolers, servicemen, surfers and beach bums. A few rocks and bottles were thrown, a few people got injured among the crowds. But by national standards, in 1964, a year dominated by race riots, urban uprisings and a blazing war in Southeast Asia, the events at the beachfront on Labor Day weekend in Seaside were fairly tame.

Race riots in New York City – the infamous Harlem Riots along with events in Rochester, New York; Jersey City, Elizabeth and Paterson, New Jersey; Dixmoor, Illinois and Philadelphia Pennsylvania, all showed far greater violence, property damage, and arrests.

During the Harlem Riots from July 18 to July 23, 1964, rioters destroyed property and looted stores after the shooting of a 15-year-old African American by a New York City police officer. In the aftermath, one more person was killed, 118 injured and 465 arrested.

By comparison, the most horrific tragedy in Oregon on Labor Day weekend didn't come from the three days of Seaside beach unrest, but a head-on crash in a small river town, killing two Washington youths, two sailors and a teenage girl.

Unlike Labor Day 1962 and 1963, at no point over the weekend did the military force of local and state police, National Guardsmen and auxiliary forces lose control. A coordinated police and military response played a big part; so did cooperation with local businessmen and officials. As the weekend passed, Seaside felt a level of security they hadn't experienced in the previous two years.

Seaside was lucky to be able to count the stores with broken windows.

Before and after the riots, Seaside Mayor Maurice Pysher bemoaned the lack of firearms used in the Seaside riots. Yet as onerous as the hickory clubs, helmets and fire hoses, none of them proved sufficient to cause a loss of life. By today's standards, both sides – young people and law enforcement – were underarmed, small city police officers and volunteers facing an "invasion" of young people flinging rocks and bottles. We can only conjecture what would have happened if guns had been added into the mix.

Victory lap

Seaside's state, police and military preparations had made a difference in containing the kids in 1964, and in the immediate aftermath of the Labor Day riots, officials patted themselves on the back.

Seaside officials wrote Governor Mark Hatfield of their "sincere appreciation to you, members of your staff, the Oregon State Police and National Guard units for the splendid assistance rendered our ocean-resort town this past Labor Day weekend. We feel that would could have been a major disaster this year was averted because of these efforts."

The *Astorian's* publisher Morgan Coe shared the post-riot compliments in a letter to the governor.

"Now that another Seaside nightmare is behind you, I want to offer my sincere congratulations for the fine job you and your helpers did last weekend," Coe wrote. "I feel you may have passed the peak of this trouble but it will linger on for years to come to some degree."

Police Superintendent Maison expressed his indebtedness to the Military Department for its "excellent housing and training facilities at Camp Rilea and to the Oregon National Guard for its valued assistance."

"It would be an oversight if we failed to mention the helicopter pilots who kept us so well informed by air observation and gave the beach throng some very anxious moments by their repeated low-level fly-overs," Maison wrote.

Relations with the press and other news media and the local authorities were "excellent," the superintendent added, thanks to the efforts of Hatfield aide Warne Nunn and military staff officers.

Hatfield did a victory lap with a visit to Seaside two weeks after Labor Day, joining Max Schafer Sr., the publisher of the weekly *Seaside Signal*, Mayor Pysher and Police Chief Healea.

Hatfield returned the gratitude "for the cooperation which you extended and your patience and understanding in a very difficult situation. I share with you a sense of pride in the manner in which state forces and the city and county personnel performed in their respective assignments."

'Whipping post'

For those of us living in a time of social media trolls and vigilante justice, the public in 1964 responded to the riots in a way that we today might recognize. Both in their viciousness and outlandishness, many people were practically unhinged by the three years of rioting.

In an election year, with America reeling from the assassination of President John F. Kennedy and on the brink of war in Asia and in the nation's cities, a sense of nervousness pervaded over Seaside as it did cities throughout the country.

What was happening?

A future hardline approach suited the *Signal*'s editorial team just fine.

The young visitors to Seaside weren't "youths" anymore – they were punks, thugs and hoodlums; they traveled in "rat packs" and "wolf packs."
Law enforcement proved this year "they meant business," the *Signal* wrote.

> "The people of Seaside owe a debt of gratitude to state officials and to the Oregon State Police. Had it not been for the presence of the state police beginning at noon Saturday, the punks would have done exactly what they threatened to do. They would have burned buildings, looted stores and destroyed many thousands of dollars worth of property. The center of Seaside would have been a schambles (sic) when they had finished. This cannot continue year after year. ... We have no desire to tell the state police how to manage their business. But it is obvious that the preparation for the difficulty must include plans for wholesale arrests."

In the period known for its chasmic generation gap, in the realm of the public commons, Seaside was an irreversible earthquake fault.
A 56-year-old Portland man wrote the governor: "Now I do not advocate shooting these kids at Seaside, but I do say, "Let's make the consequences for these acts of violence so severe that when these kids return to Seaside they come only to swim, have good clean fun and spend money."
No proposal was considered too extreme for those who hoped to put the genie back in the bottle and turn back the clock to a different America.
Send the young people to Vietnam, wrote a Beaverton man. "I would suggest that when you arrest anyone, regardless of age in one of these riots, that he be told that he will be inducted into the army and without training be sent into the actual fighting."
Another offered this method of punishment: "I once read where Canada still used the whipping post," they wrote, adding: "Their crime rate was nil."
Resident Dorothy Crum suggested that the police "have the right to do something drastic," although she didn't spell out what that might entail.
This letter-writer's longhand note suggested: "The deep South once had what was called a chain gang. No three meals a day and a warm place to sleep at night. Once a person was off that gang, he never wanted to return again."

Other contributors to the op-ed pages had a wide array of imaginative ideas on how to turn Battleground Seaside into the popular family destination it once was.

Instead of the whip, they should use education, religion and more wholesome pastimes than carousing aimlessly along the Prom.

Robert Witt of Seattle suggested the city of Seaside adopt an urban renewal plan to "get rid of its honky-tonk appearance and perhaps develop a space age theme with an annual award honoring the world's top space scientist."

Dr. Irving Roddy, speaking for the Oregon Council of Alcohol Problems, urged the city to "prepare a constructive program activity" that will bring "both energy and money" to the city.

These could include a dance floor for square dancing, a preschool football program and a Sunday morning worship service, "Youth for Christ."

N.E. Smith of Salem suggested that when a minor is arrested, their parents' names made public. "Discipline should be in the high chair, not the electric chair," they wrote.

Thomas Morgan of Forest Grove suggested a prohibition on liquor and gambling to fight the "lawless drinking gangs." (Nunn responded: "Prohibition was an interesting experiment but in my opinion was a miserable failure.")

Warren Jones of Beaverton wanted them to be "sent to the war fronts immediately without training." "If they want to fight, let's put them where their fighting will do some good."

"I think desperate measures should be taken this time," wrote one family. "If arrested, why not slave labor?"

A University of Oregon student, James Norton protested the public reaction was being driven by "blind emotionalism."

Norton wrote the governor: "Where I expect to see constructive suggestions for improvement of the situation, I find instead such statements as 'There's no logical explanation,' 'They're just punks,' 'Throw the punks in jail,' 'Throw their parents in jail,' or 'Expose them to public humiliation.' Such statements are made in anger and frustration and show no attempts on the parts of their authors to understand the problem."

W.G. Frick, age 90, also urged tolerance. Frick suggested young folks might be interested in a "salmon bake" in Seaside.

"Severe punishment," he wrote, "will only make them mean."

Columbia Avenue in Philadelphia, Pennsylvania, following riots in 1964.

BLACK RIOTS, WHITE RIOTS

In the aftermath of Labor Day 1964 Seaside's riots were swallowed up by the nation's race riots. And like Seaside, beach towns like Hampton Beach, New Hampshire, and Ocean City, Maryland, were all too delighted to be overshadowed by the violent urban warfare in America's black ghettos. Rioters in summer vacation towns would go back to college in the fall; some would suffer for their temporary miscreancy; others would enlist or be drafted to the war in Vietnam. Those fighting in the ghettos were condemned to continue their battles throughout the '60s and beyond. A rock 'n' roll concert on the beach wouldn't put out the fires in America's cities.

Despite the difference in causes and responses to the 1964 riots nationwide, in a presidential election year, politicians were quick to seize on the issue as a source of fear. U.S. Senator Barry Goldwater, the Republican candidate, prepared a film showing the polarity of the nation.

"Choice" is sprinkled with images of an America at a crossroads, a nation where it is police who are "handcuffed," not the lawbreakers.

Newspaper columnist and historian Gary Wills wrote the film presented "a glimpse of America sinking into a pit of sex and violence under the patronage of Lyndon Johnson."

Using footage from riots across the nation, including Seaside, Oregon, home of three consecutive years of youth riots, Goldwater described "justice as a sick joke," with "more and more criminals turned loose on the street." This was the new "take what you can America," riddled with burglary, rape, muggings and murder: "Here, now, in the very shadow of the fast deal operators."

In the new America, the ancient moral law is mocked, incanted the narrator. "One nation under God ... who's He?"

In the past eight months – the spring and summer of 1964 – they warned, there were more riots in the United States than in the past eight years.

The country, the narrator cried, was governed by "mobocracy."

In a fascinating analysis, "The FBI and the Politics of the Riots, 1964-1968" in the *Journal of American History*, author Kenneth O'Reilly described Goldwater's attempts on a national level to capitalize on the apparent breakdown of law and order that threatened to cost Lyndon Johnson the election.

Johnson sought to counter the Republican's charges of lawlessness before the November election. He asked FBI chief J. Edgar Hoover to put together a report on the past year's unrest. He even had a prominent Republican, former presidential candidate and prosecutor Thomas E. Dewey, put the FBI memos on the riots into a final draft.

When the report was delivered on Sept. 26, 1964 – weeks before the November presidential election – Seaside was included among America's nine riot locations. The report recognized the "demoralizing conditions in which much of the Negro population lives" as an element leading to the race riots."

Finding common elements between the inner city riots and those of the resort towns may seem a bit of a stretch. But Dewey and his team did thread common factors between America's urban riots and those in the white vacation towns of Seaside and Hampton Beach.

All were a senseless attack on all constituted authority without purpose or object, Dewey wrote. Rioting "reflects an increasing breakdown across the nation in respect for the law and the rights of other people to be secure in their property."

The report divided the nine riots into the seven major city riots and the two beach city riots, Seaside and Hampton Beach.

In each of the urban riots, according to the report, a conflict with a policeman often ignited the violence. "As mob spirit swept through the crowd it became increasingly unruly, began stoning police officers and civilians and the ominous surge of a mass of violent people bent on destruction spread through the streets."

Complete defiance of the law and the rights of others grew and fed upon itself, according to the report.

Mob action grew, rocks and ash cans were hurled from rooftops. Molotov cocktails and fire bombs were thrown, usually on the second or third day of the riots. Looting followed.

"Adults were found in riot areas carrying furniture away on their backs, television sets, as well as more easily portable articles. In some sections the looting was carried on actively by women and even children."

The riots at Hampton Beach and Seaside involved groups made up predominantly of young whites on the Labor Day weekend. Disturbances had occurred at these beaches on previous holidays but this year the riot at Hampton Beach was much more serious, causing many injuries and great damage. According to reports, the rioters lit trash cans on fire, overturned cars and a phone booth, and smashed windows. Some of them began throwing rocks at police officers.

At Seaside, effective police planning kept the damage to a minimum. The two riots, more than 3,200 miles apart on both coasts – resulted in 256 arrests.

> "In each case, there were reports of advance preparation for the riot. The individuals involved ranged from youths in their late teens whose vacation was coming to an end to toughs and other hoodlums, in their middle 20s, whose conduct indicated a purpose to make trouble and profit by it. Whatever the original intent of the majority, the riots were not the innocent exuberance of youth but were persistent, prolonged and violent."

The majority of the FBI report's conclusions focused on urban unrest. But there were some universal lessons to be learned that could include all nine cities, including Seaside and Hampton Beach.
The report issued among their conclusions:

- A common characteristic of the riots was a senseless attack on all constituted authority without purpose or object.
- While adult troublemakers often incited the riots, the mob violence was dominated by the acts of youths ranging in age up to the middle twenties. They were variously characterized by responsible people as "school dropouts," "young punks," "common hoodlums" and "drunken kids."
- The breakdown of respect of law and order could be attributed to "an immunity to public exposure for serious offenses and often the absence of punishment of any kind."

Another commonality was the media equation: the arrival of large numbers of reporters and television cameras at the riots provided an opportunity "for self-seeking individuals to publicize wild charges on television and radio and in the press."
"These circumstances provided additional incitement to the rioters and served to attract others to the scene," wrote Dewey and his team.
Interesting that this was the year Marshall McLuhan published *Understanding Media*, and the introduction of his famed phrase, "The medium is the message."

Moral choices in Oregon
As Washington, D.C., went, so did Oregon. Law and order was the dominant issue in the state that fall. That raised some thorny moral issues on protest and human rights.
A speech given by Nunn, the mayor's assistant, at the East Side Commercial Club, a business group, at the Sheraton Motor Inn in Portland met the topic head-on.
Nunn told club members mass civil disobedience – by any race or group – is actually "encouragement for lawlessness."
He accused clergymen leading "what are billed as peaceful demonstrations" as carrying "the seeds of violence."

Governor Hatfield doubled down: "If clergymen take part in civil disobedience, they must extend the right to everyone to disobey any law they do not like."

The "beach blanket bingo" crowd was giving way to "Alice's Restaurant" and "Midnight Cowboy."

The race riots and burgeoning antiwar movement referenced by the clergy addressed moral and ethical issues of the 1960s: the repression of African Americans and the sacrifice of American youth on foreign soil.

Progressive clergymen and women in Oregon wanted the governor to acknowledge critical differences.

To members of the Greater Portland Council of Churches, Nunn and Hatfield were missing a crucial point. Beyond the Oregon Coast and a few beach communities in the Northeast, the youth riots had reached their expiration date – replaced by the war in Vietnam, Timothy Leary and hard rock.

Race riots were only the latest chapter in America's historic divide.

In correspondence with the governor, the Lower Columbia Association of Conservative Baptists stood on record supporting the stand by Hatfield and Nunn condemning the actions of "ministers and religious leaders who have led and are leading so-called peaceful, nonviolent protests and demonstrations in the area of civil rights, but which in reality carry the seeds of violence and civil disobedience."

Liberal clergy, however, were quick to point out the differences, warning from an establishment organization that the response was more nuanced.

Charles Foster of the First Methodist Church in Corning, New York, wrote to the University of Oregon alumni journal seeking clarification of Nunn's statements on law and morality.

Nunn assumes "an immoral society making immoral laws should not be challenged by the nation's citizens concerned about right," Foster wrote. This is not necessarily true, as is obviously seen in racially discriminatory clauses in many of our laws. I question the validity of both assumptions."

Civil disobedience "in its best forms," Foster wrote, may awaken both the government and the church to their respective responsibilities in today's world. "The riots may also awaken the governing agencies of our society who make the laws, and the churches to the fact that neither have provided the training ground for many of our youth in discovering meaning and purpose in a contemporary social context."

It is a question of disobeying laws in particular – "disobedience rooted in a high moral order."

Members of the Christian Social Concerns Committee echoed these comments. "Where there is no recourse to the ballot to effect abrogation of such laws, responsible disobedience effectively brings about their ultimate appeal... Something has to give when a significant section of our population has suffered intolerable treatment. Peaceful demonstrations are one way of channeling this indignation constructively."

Robert Burtner of the Methodist Church in Salem wrote Governor Hatfield that the participation by clergy in acts of civil disobedience comes at the end of a hard road of "considerable soul-searching, hard work and attempted conciliation."

When a clergyman does reach the point where his alternative leads only through disobeying unjust laws, we "have little right to publicly castigate him," Burtner wrote.

Representatives of the Greater Portland Council of Churches shared a similar message:

> "If the church is indifferent to what the state or any other human grouping does to people, even though it does this on the ground of being 'spiritual,' it denies God's concern for his children. That concern, as we understand it, has everything to do with social, economic and political processes, because it is always a call to social concern: to feed the hungry, clothe the naked, and otherwise minister to the most elemental and material of human needs."

The pastor at the Westminster Presbyterian Church in Portland advised the governor and his assistant Nunn they had "seriously mistaken ideas of the church's mission."

> "The gravity of your position on civil rights demonstrations against laws believed to be unconstitutional is, first of all, that your position is based upon personal inclination and not upon facts. We respectfully call to your attention the now completed investigations by the Federal Bureau of investigation of nine riots including Seaside. The FBI gives no indication that civil rights

demonstrations participated in by members of the clergy lead to riots. On the contrary, the FBI found, 'In most of the communities, respected Negro and other civic leaders, clergymen, and public officials made every effort to halt the riots.'"

A Methodist pastor, Lorenz Schultz, suggested "Many more people than you might wish are aware of this matter and are concerned over your silence about reconsidering or redefining your remarks. I would hope that a clarification would be coming soon."
Nunn countered that "a sanction to civil disobedience can readily be misinterpreted to be a right of defiance of law under the individual's own terms."
Nunn did relinquish some ground in response to Schultz:

> "I want to carefully draw a distinction between peaceful demonstrations which are perfectly proper and in order, and deliberate violation of law under the nice title of civil disobedience. While recognizing the role of peaceful demonstration and accepting its value, I feel that we should not tolerate civil disobedience – that is – the deliberation violation of the law ... We have the necessary avenues and processes by law to accomplish our goals and to realize the reforms which we need."

An article in the *FBI Law Enforcement Bulletin* in 1965, elaborated on the theme, also conflating both "white riots" and the nation's race riots.
Whatever the factors may be, "hair-trigger situations build up in which some minor incident sets hundreds and often thousands of Americans on a law-defying rampage in which lives are destroyed and countless millions of dollars of property is damaged or looted."

Governor Mark Hatfield, second from left, meets with *Signal* publisher Max Schafer, Mayor Maurice Pysher and Chief Ken Healea on Sept. 17, 1964.

THE PEOPLE HAVE SPOKEN

Police contained 1964's Labor Day riots in Seaside without serious incident. Officials wanted to keep it that way in 1965.

But the three years of unrest led to a sea change at city hall and town governance.

After three years of a tumultuous ride as Seaside mayor, Maurice Pysher initially announced he would not run. He had a change of heart when a preferred candidate opted out, but missed the Oct. 2 deadline in doing so. He ran as a write-in candidate. Candidate Elvin "Al" Goodman, a sitting member of the City Council, sought the office. A retired gas company manager and former state president of the Oregon Moose association, Goodman was a member of the musicians union.

Pysher's last-minute write-in bid mustered a surprising 750 votes, about three-quarters of Goodman's tally. Pysher clearly remained popular among many of his constituents.

Pysher pledged his support for the new mayor.

"The apparent results of this city election plainly show that the people have spoken," he said in a statement. "Who are we or any one of us to feel that we are so wedded to our own judgment as to what is in the best public interest as to be reluctant in abiding with the democratic principles or majority rule."

Goodman, in return, said he would "work for the best interest of the city and its people. I feel that we all owe Mayor Pysher a vote of thanks for the work that he has done for the city the past four years."

As he took office in January 1965, Goodman sought to put the riots behind the city. "I want to make one thing clear," he said. "What's passed is passed. I'm not interested in digging up anything that happened in the past. There's only one way that Seaside can go, and that is ahead. There's only one side, so far as I'm concerned, and that is Seaside."

Riot playbook

The successful efforts of 1964 held promise for law enforcement. Governor Mark Hatfield, by now experienced in beach riot control, had developed a stable team to meet future unrest.

Officials met at Camp Rilea – the military base about 10 miles north of Seaside – on April 21 to begin plans for Labor Day 1965.

Many of the same faces returned: Oregon State Police Superintendent Maison, Warne Nunn, army Major General Donald Anderson, and Clatsop County Sheriff Carl Bondietti.

Using the 1964 response as a model, the joint security force divided the city into zones. State police would monitor downtown; city police would patrol residential district; and county police would cover neighboring cities. The National Guard would provide rooftop security where needed along Broadway, transport prisoners from Seaside to Astoria, guard the Seaside power plant, aid in communications, furnish helicopters for observation and jeeps for whatever beach patrolling might be required.

The city remained cautiously optimistic, hopeful to avoid a repeat of the chaos of 1962 and 1963.

A few 'kibitzers'

Young people weren't allowed on Broadway on Saturday; only police, officials and members of the press were granted access.

Teenagers clustered around on the Prom or on neighboring cross streets, talking and joking with police. It was described as a jovial, sometimes joyful bunch.

All that changed early Saturday night. About 75 young people gathered on the beach and for a bonfire. They began recruiting more young people, yelling to onlookers on the Promenade: "Bring more wood!"

But the party never got started.

Oregon State Police rushed to the Prom and prevented any of the spectators from joining the group at the fire.

Two jeeps filled with guardsmen rumbled toward the group from the ocean side, their headlights lighting up the scene. Guardsmen armed with rifles ordered the young people off the beach.

Eighty-one people were arrested on minor charges and alcohol confiscated by local authorities, most charged with alcohol possession or disturbing the peace.

"No violence or resistance was reported," the *Oregonian* wrote. "Near midnight police were busy dispersing small groups of teenagers which reassembled as soon as officers passed, mostly in front of a teenage night club."

The riots still made the front pages. But the headlines were mild – in the *Oregonian*, buried in a single column tucked into the first page, no photo. The news – to the great relief of Seaside residents and businesses – was tame.

"Sixteen teenagers were arrested Saturday night by police who patrolled Seaside in an attempt to prevent another Labor Day weekend riot."

Sunday turned up "no incident of major consequence," the *Signal* reported. "A few kibitzers made faint attempts to rile the police, but were soon discouraged."

"The consensus is the three-year stretch of Labor Day weekend riots by youthful visitors is broken for good," wrote the *Oregonian*.

Governor Hatfield addressed the press through his aide, Nunn, speaking to reporters at the Seasider Hotel. "We are encouraged by the responsible attitude taken by our youth during this Labor Day weekend. I believe this attitude will prevail and that this is the turning point which will again see the coastal resort area a place for family recreation."

"It is our opinion," wrote the *Signal* immediately after the holiday, "that the pattern of the last three years has been broken and we need fear riots no longer. However, the city must, over a period of one or two years, maintain a show of force, to make sure the cure is permanent. We must not be lulled into the idea that it can't happen to us again, because the riots can, and will, if they are allowed to happen."

Seaside jail, now a tourist attraction at Seaside Brewery.

Epilogue

And what of the characters of those days?

Governor Mark O. Hatfield occupied the national stage for decades as the U.S. Senator from Oregon, a seat he held for 30 years. A political moderate, he rejected Goldwater's conservative platform and later the hawkish stance on the war in Vietnam. An author who married faith with his political philosophy, he concerned himself a moderate. As the Republican party veered to the right he was an outlier, voting against President Ronald Reagan's MX Missile plan and a co-sponsor of nuclear freeze legislation.

Hatfield's assistant, Warne Nunn, followed Hatfield in Washington, D.C., upon his election in 1966. He returned to Oregon where he worked for Pacific Power and Light in Portland in various executive roles. He died in 2007.

Maurice Pysher left the job of mayor in December 1964 and lived his days of retirement out of the public eye.

Elvin "Al" Goodman presided over the new city manager style government for more than a decade, ushering in additional changes to the city including a new convention center project.

The Pypo Club, located in a former electric company building on Oceanway, provided a musical venue for teens from the 1960s and 1970s.

Many of the bands that played there, including the Kingsmen, Paul Revere and the Raiders, and the Fabulous Wailers, leaped to the top of the national and regional charts. Local musicians and bands always found a home on stage there. I am told many local couples met, wooed and married after meeting at the Pypo Club. "Rockin' Roberts" himself died in a tragic 1967 car accident after leaving a party.

In part inspired by the contentious City Hall experience of the last three years, in November 1964 the city voted to adopt a city manager form of municipal government. This would replace the mayor – an elected, unpaid volunteer – as the prime decision-maker in the city's daily affairs.

The city manager, noted the new mayor, would be charged to see that all city laws and ordinances would be enforced, appoint and remove department heads and employees and prepare the budget, among other responsibilities.

The city was joining a statewide trend, modeling their amendment to follow the terms and provision incorporated in a model city manager charter by the League of Oregon Cities.

In an editorial, the *Signal* wrote: "We are convinced that the adoption of the city manager plan, under conditions which would permits success, would be of great benefit to Seaside. Most of the troubles which we have experienced in the past could be eliminated and we could be confident of avoiding them in the future."

The charter initiative for a city manager form of government succeeded by a nearly 2-1 margin. The city did respond and took steps to both the city's image and its options for families and young people.

Turning the page

Seaside was eager to turn its back on the three years of Labor Day riots. Business opportunities beckoned, and the past could not be a prelude to the future.

In 1965, the *Seaside Signal* reported on a proposed convention center to make the county the "premier beach resort on the north Pacific Coast… nothing to compare with it north of San Francisco."

A location had not yet been chosen, but the *Signal* wrote, "it is obvious that it could only be located in the Seaside area, where it would serve Seaside, Gearhart and Cannon Beach."

A committee proposed a center that could hold more than 1,000 people, and could be used for the Miss Oregon pageant, music events and theater festivals. "Uses for the building would be limitless, the committee feels."

A new convention center opened on First Avenue along the Necanicum River in 1971. It recently celebrated 50 years and a renovation. The center is booked past 2030.

Police Chief Ken Healea asked voters to support construction of a new police station and jail — undoubtedly a result of the overcrowding in the cells during the Seaside riots. "The size and condition of our present jail is at a point of urgency such that the only practical solution is the construction of a new jail building."

In years to come, taxpayers funded a new city hall, police station and fire station. The former city hall, police station and jail are now occupied by Seaside Brewery, overseen by proprietor Jimmy Griffin, who has taken pains to retain the building's unique character.

As the Seaside Chamber of Commerce and civic groups wooed businesses back to Seaside, those three years of 1962, 1963 and 1964 became closeted history.

It is a sign of how quickly they vanished that in the *Seaside Signal*'s 1990 retrospective, "75 years of the *Seaside Signal*," recounting the newspaper's history from 1905, among the 92 articles included highlighting notable events, not one mention of the Seaside Labor Day riots of 1962, 1963 and 1964.

Former city officials have acknowledged that there was an unwritten rule to stay mum — not too difficult in a transient community of vacationers and retirees.

Another riot — in 1999 — took headlines briefly, a "girls gone wild" scenario in which filmmakers riled up a Saturday afternoon crowd.

Between 200 and 300 spring break revelers, mostly high school and college students, gathered on the Prom in front of the Turnaround.

Beginning with a drunken brawl, it eventually involved 200 teens and college-aged students roughing up the town.

A bonfire was lit; the crowd grew and young people tore fixtures from the restrooms. Police used smoke to disperse the crowd. Reinforcements came from the state police, the sheriff's department and the Oregon Liquor Control Commission. More than 50 officers were deployed.

Downtown windows had 14 windows smashed, the *Signal* reported.

Tear gas was deployed, law enforcement donned riot gear, and 20 people arrested. One officer suffered a broken ankle and another needed stitches after being hit with a rock.

"The police exercised huge restraint," city manager Gene Miles told the *Signal* at the time. "The young people had a little too much alcohol and got carried away."

This riot seemed one of exuberance, opportunism and bad judgment.

The following week there were 50 state, county and local police watching the city streets.

Since that time Seaside has worked to solidify its reputation as a family destination, not a youth party town, with many notable exceptions.

"Our community took it very seriously," Sunset Empire Park and Recreation District director Mary Blake said in 2004 of the 1999 incident.

> "We got together and formed a spring break committee, and we worked for years to be proactive and define a protocol for when people come here. 'You're a guest in the community, and we want you, and we want you to recognize that basic manners are expected.'"

The problems that accompany underage drinking are "hard on a community," Blake added.

The city took the approach that the behavior "wasn't healthy, wasn't cool," she said. "We said, 'We're going to set parameters and expectations and let it be known that it's not a party community where people are underage and unsupervised.'"

'They came to riot'

In September 1965, the state prepared what was to be the final word on the subject, a riot report prepared for the Office of Juvenile Deliquency and Youth Development from the Welfare Administration, a division of the Department of Health, Education and Welfare.

The report, preparted by Ken Polk, Bert Romo and Daniel Knapp, outlined political and social changes leading to the riots.

Although Seaside for decades had dealt with vacationing crowds that at times surpassed, 50,000, these were the first instances of rioting in the city's history, they wrote.

How, the report's authors wrote, could they have reacted differently?

> "Making the decisions necessary to prevent riots may not be an easy task for the city government to accomplish. Very often it may require a series of 'negotiations' which take on the appearance of an unacceptable compromise. In all probability, however, in most cases a range of alternatives are available which will prevent these youth outbreaks. It is unfortunate that the alternatives which might have prevented these disturbances were never given serious consideration by the city of Seaside."

Could it have those three years of unrest been stopped?
Probably not, Polk concluded.
The youth came to Seaside to riot, and they did riot.

Selected Bibliography

Andrews, Silvie. "Material Witness, the Seaside Riots of 1962-1964." *Oregon Historic Quarterly*, vol. 121, no. 3, 2020.

Blecha, Peter. *Sonic Boom: The History of Northwest Rock, from Louie Louie to Smells Like Teen Spirit,* London, U.K.: Backbeat Books, 2009.

Craig, David. *The Louie Files: '62 Seaside Riot.* https://portlandorbit.com/category/the-louie-files/.

Gaston, Helen. "Oney: A Legend in her Time." *Cumtux. Clatsop County Historical Society Quarterly.* Vol. 13, No. 2, Spring 1993, by Helen Gaston, p. 6.

Lucia, Ellis. *The Big Blow: The Story of the Pacific Northwest's Columbus Day Storm.* Berkeley, California: Overland West Press, 1967.

McKenna, Hugh. "The 1962 Seaside Labor Day Riot." *Cumtux. Clatsop County Historical Society Quarterly*, vol. 17, no. 3, (summer 2017).

Manolides, Jimmy. *The Louie Report*. http://pnwbands.com/olympics.html.

Marsh, Dave. *Louie Louie: The History and Mythology of the World's Most Famous Rock 'n Roll Song.* New York: Hyperion, 1995.

O'Reilly, Kenneth. "The FBI and the Politics of the Riots, 1964-1968." *The Journal of American History*, vol. 75, no. 1, 1988.

Polk, Ken. *The Seaside Riots.* prepared for the Office of Juvenile Delinquency and Youth Development, Welfare Administration, Department of Health, Education and Welfare, Sept. 1965. With Bert Romo and Daniel Knapp.

Regan, Col, Joseph L. "Let's Have a Riot." *FBI Law Enforcement Bulletin*, April 1965, Vol. 34, No. 4.

Newspapers: *Seaside Signal*, *The Daily Astorian*, *The New York Times*, *Oregon Journal*, *Oregon Statesman*, the *Oregonian*, *Eugene Register-Guard*, United Press International.

Photos courtesy City of Seaside; *Seaside Signal*; the *Oregonian*; Mark O. Hatfield Library at Willamette University; Seaside Police; Seaside Museum & Historical Society; Oregon Military Museum; Clatsop County Historical Society.
Cover photo, the *Oregonian*, page one, Sept. 2, 1962.
Back cover author photo by Eve Marx.

Acknowledgments

This project began as a result of the intense interest from my fellow Seasiders in this "secret" city past. So to all those locals near and far who showed an interest in the Seaside riots, thank you for sharing your memories.

Particular thanks goes to Steve Wright, president of the Seaside Museum and Historical Society; special thanks to Leah Griffith and Teresa Taylor for their early encouragement.

Same goes for the staff of the Seaside Library, including former director Esther Moberg, director Jennifer Reading and assistant director Josh Moorman.

Thank you to Kim Jordan of City Hall, who opened up the secret "second floor" of city archives for my research. Same to Police Chief Dave Ham who shared police reports and correspondence from the period. Seaside Fire Chief Joey Daniels offered insights into the department then and now.

Our story took us to the Oregon Military Museum in Happy Valley, Oregon, and the Mark O. Hatfield Library at Willamette University in Salem. His correspondence proved essential in writing this book. Thank you to those librarians for their assistance.

Dozens of Seasiders shared their thoughts in person or on social media. Ky Weed Jennings of Seaside Friends Facebook page provided encouragement and true inside information from the git-go – stuff no non-native Seasider could ever hope to understand.

Gratitude for first-hand accounts goes to Cheryl Adamscheck, Doug Barker, Dallas Cook, Karen Emmerling, Mark Hansen, Tom Horning, Joyce Hunt, Larry Kriegshauser, Jeanne Nordmark, Jeff Roehm, Jim Roehm, Curt Sagner Jr., John Spence and Craig Weston. Special thanks to Jimmy Griffin of Seaside Brewery for his insider tour of the old jail.

Special thanks to writer friends Laurie Lewis and Neil Wexler for their invaluable input. My cousin David Plaut gave me encouragement every step of the way. Being married to a writer and writing teacher doesn't hurt when one is at a loss for words. As am I in thanking Eve Marx.

About the Author

R.J. Marx is an author, editor and journalist.

At the *Record-Review* newspaper in Bedford, New York, he won numerous awards for his journalism, including the New York Press Association's awards for the state's best community newspaper.

In 2015, he relocated to the Oregon Coast, where he was the editor of the *Seaside Signal* until 2023. His experience covering Oregon's North Coast introduced him to the people and historical events of Seaside in the 1960s.

He lives in Seaside with his wife Eve and their dogs Lucy and Trixie.

www.ingramcontent.com/pod-product-compliance
Lightning Source LLC
Chambersburg PA
CBHW051948290426
44110CB00015B/2154